THE INDIAN CHRISTIANS OF ST. THOMAS

THE
INDIAN CHRISTIANS OF ST. THOMAS

OTHERWISE CALLED

THE SYRIAN CHRISTIANS OF MALABAR

A Sketch of their History, and an Account of their Present Condition, as well as a Discussion of the Legend of St. Thomas

BY

THE REV. W. J. RICHARDS, D. D.

WITH A PREFACE BY EUGENE STOCK, ESQ.

GYAN

Published by

GYAN

Gyan Publishing House
5, Ansari Road
Daryaganj, New Delhi-110002
Phone: 011-47034999, 9811692060
E-mail: books@gyanbooks.com

Distribution Network
gyanbooks.com
India, USA, Canada, UK, Australia

ISBN: 978-93-6208-128-5 (PB)
First Published, 1908

2nd Impression 2024

Printed at: Gyan Press, Delhi.

THE INDIAN CHRISTIANS OF ST. THOMAS
Author: W. J. RICHARDS, WITH A PREFACE BY EUGENE STOCK

THE INDIAN CHRISTIANS OF ST. THOMAS

THE MOST REV. MAR THOMAS ATHANASIUS.

The Second Reforming Metran or Metropolitan.
Succeeded 1877. Died 1893.

THE INDIAN CHRISTIANS OF ST. THOMAS

OTHERWISE CALLED

THE SYRIAN CHRISTIANS OF MALABAR

A Sketch of their History, and an Account of their Present Condition, as well as a Discussion of the Legend of St. Thomas

BY

THE REV. W. J. RICHARDS, D.D.

Thirty-five years C.M.S. Missionary to the Hindus in Travancore and Cochin
Hon. Chaplain to the Bishop

WITH A PREFACE BY EUGENE STOCK, ESQ.

Author of *The History of the Church Missionary Society*

LONDON
BEMROSE & SONS LIMITED, 4 SNOW HILL, E.C.
AND DERBY
1908

This little book is dedicated to HIS GRACE THE RIGHT HONOURABLE AND MOST REVEREND RANDALL THOMAS DAVIDSON, D.D., Lord Archbishop of Canterbury, Primate of All England—the friend of the Assyrian Christians—as a token of humble respect; and to the RIGHT REVEREND NOEL HODGES, D.D., Rector of St. Cuthbert's, Bedford, Assistant Bishop of Ely and Honorary Canon of the Cathedral, during fifteen years Bishop of Travancore and Cochin — the constant friend of the Jacobite and the Reformed Syrians of Malabar (partly of the same stock as the Assyrians) — in acknowledgment of the greatest possible kindness received from his lordship by the Author

PREFACE

AT the request of my friend, the author of this book, I write these few lines to introduce him and his work. Dr. Richards has been a missionary of the Church Missionary Society in Travancore since 1871. He was at different times Vice-Principal of the Society's College at Cottayam, Principal of the Cambridge Nicholson Theological and Training Institution at the same place, and Missionary-in-Charge of at least three of the Mission districts. He was one of the revisers of the Malayalam Bible, the chief reviser of the Prayer Book in the same language, and for these important services Archbishop Temple conferred on him the Lambeth D.D. He was also editor of the *Travancore Diocesan Gazette*. He has well studied the past history of the ancient Syrian Church of Malabar, and has been intimately cognizant of its various divisions and developments in recent years.

All this I can say of the author, and I could say more were it necessary. Of his book I have no authority to speak—it speaks for itself. It is obviously based on first-hand knowledge, and contains much important and curious information.

These ancient Churches of the East deserve our sympathy, and I trust the present work may awaken much interest in the Syrians of Travancore.

They were for centuries a light in a dark place—a feeble light it is true, but one which we cannot but believe that it pleased God to use.

EUGENE STOCK.

March 7th, 1908.

CONTENTS

CHAPTER I.

PAGE

THE CHRISTIANS AND THEIR EXTERNALS . . . 1

CHAPTER II.

ST. THOMAS—THE NESTORIANS—ROME—REVOLT . 10

CHAPTER III.

MORE CHANGES — ALLIANCE WITH ENGLISH — RUPTURE 17

CHAPTER IV.

THE REMNANT—A WYCLIF—THE REFORMATION . 28

CHAPTER V.

A REFORMING METROPOLITAN—AN EXCOMMUNICATING PATRIARCH 36

CHAPTER VI.

THE REFORMERS WIN TRUTH AND LOSE LAWSUITS 45

CHAPTER VII.

THE JACOBITES—THE REFORMERS AT LIBERTY—SOME ROMANS 52

CHAPTER VIII.

CHIEFLY ABOUT BISHOPS 62

PAGE

CHAPTER IX.

A DISCUSSION—SOUTH INDIA AND ST. THOMAS . 65

CHAPTER X.

THE INDIAN STORY OF ST. THOMAS 72

CHAPTER XI.

EARLY WRITERS AND KING ALFRED 78

CHAPTER XII.

INDIAN STORY CONTINUED 82

CHAPTER XIII.

AN OBJECTION DISCUSSED 89

CHAPTER XIV.

SPECIMENS 95

CHAPTER XV.

MANUSCRIPTS, SYRIAC AND MALAYALAM, AND THE PRINTED TRANSLATIONS OF THE SCRIPTURES . 102

CHAPTER XVI.

THE PRESENT AND THE FUTURE 112

APPENDIX

BISHOP WILSON'S CHARGE, 1843 118

GLOSSARY 135

BIBLIOGRAPHY 137

ILLUSTRATIONS

Most Rev. Mar Thomas Athanasius . . . *Frontispiece*

Map of Travancore . . . . *facing page* 1

PAGE

Cherya (Little or Later) Church, Cottayam 3

Snapshot of two Bishops in a boat 6

A Group of Syrian Girls in Miss Baker's School, Cottayam 8

Ancient Granite Slab and Inscription 11

Malabar Village Scene 16

The Bazaar, Kunnankulàm, in Native Cochin . . . 29

A Side View of the C.M.S. College Hall, Cottayam . 33

The Baker Memorial High School for Girls, Cottayam 34

Most Rev. Mar Dionysius V. 40

River near Cottayam 42

Reformed Metropolitan, with Kattarazand Deacons . 47

Landing Place, Cottayam 55

Group of Six Jacobite Metrans 63

"Old Church" Steps 76

Bridge near Olesha, Cottayam 97

A Kore-Episcopa 100

Syriac Manuscript Gospel 103

First Printed Malayalam Gospel 104

PAGE
Second Printed Malayalam Gospel 106
Malayalam Manuscript Gospel . . . 107
Final Revision of New Testament 109
Rubbing of Ancient Syro-Chinese Monument . . 110
Syrian Family 115
Anglican Pro-Cathedral, Cottayam, Holy Trinity . . 131

INTRODUCTION

IN putting together the following account of the Syrians in Malabar, the difficulty has not been to find material, but to keep back much that crowds in upon the mind of picturesque and even tragic interest.

There is extant a volume of over four hundred pages, published in England in 1694, being the Acts of the Synod, 1599, held to enforce the Syrian submission to Rome. In this book is given the ritual of the occasion—how, for instance, "the most illustrious and Reverend Lord Dom Frey Aleixo de Menezes, Archbishop Metropolitan of Goa and the Oriental parts, and, the See being vacant, of the said bishopric" (of the St. Thomas Christians), "having robed himself in his pontificals, but without his mitre, kneeling down before the altar, and having laid his hands upon the Cross that was upon a book of the Gospels, did, in his own name, as the present Prelate and Metropolitan of the Diocese, *and in the name of all the Christians belonging to the same, and every person thereof,* secular and ecclesiastic, make profession and oath of the Faith following," to wit, the Nicene Creed and the Creed of Trent, and submission, *for salvation*, to the Pope.

I might have taken from Buchanan's *Christian Researches*, 1806, delightful conversations held with the Syrian Metropolitan of that day. *The Lives of Bishops Middleton and Wilson of Calcutta* contain interesting accounts of their dealings with the Syrians eighty years ago. There is the sadly dramatic drowning of our Poet-Bishop Heber when *en route* for Travancore to smooth the way of a Metropolitan from Antioch. There are one's own recollections of people who knew Travancore in 1816, and details of more modern days. But being desirous to gratify Christian love and hope with a view of what our Church has done by the Church Missionary Society, to quicken an ancient branch of Christ's Church, I have passed over many things, pleasant and unpleasant, curious and historical, in order to give a correct, if condensed, view of the reformation movement in the Syrian Church of Malabar. And I think it is the first that has so far been given.

It is just a hundred years since the famous visit

of Rev. Claudius Buchanan, D.D., who introduced the Syrians to the Church of England.

In the following I have had advice on one point from the Venerable John Caley, for many years Archdeacon of Cottayam, and Commissary of the Diocese at various times; and no one is better able to form a judgment of matters "Syrian," for he has lived in their very midst from 1871 to 1905.

There are as few names as possible mentioned in this account, for my aim has been to give the story of the reformation among the St. Thomas Christians as simply as possible.

It was my privilege for several years to have close personal acquaintance with the Reforming Metran, Mar Matthew Athanasius, and his immediate successor, the gentle Mar Thomas Athanasius. Latterly, though living in the same country, my opportunities of meeting the present Metropolitan of the Reformed Church, Mar Titus Thoma, and his suffragan, Mar Titus Thoma II., were few, for I was living on the opposite side of "the backwater," including rivers, a two days' journey, though not more than twenty miles as the crow flies. Still, the Syrian Church diocesan monthlies, Reformed and Jacobite, were continuously at hand.

I have had many friends among the Kattanars of both sections, and I have known some of the Roman Syrian clergy and laity.

It has been my privilege to know intimately, in the capacity of teacher and co-worker, many Syrians whose fathers joined the Anglican Church seventy years ago.

In this popular account I pass over some episodes connected with the Jacobite Church which I have handled in the *Guardian* newspaper of January 7th, 1903, and thereabouts, and in the *Statement for the Anglican Episcopate*, 1904, signed by Archdeacon Caley and myself. (This has been graciously acknowledged by the Chaplain to the Archbishop of Canterbury; and the Most Reverend the Presiding Bishop, Dr. Tuttle, of the Anglican Church, U.S.A., and the Most Reverend the Bishop of Calcutta, Primate of India and Ceylon, have sent me cordial thanks.) I have also written on the same subjects in the *Indian Church News*, January, 1906, and in the January number of *The East and the West*, 1908. I have had also a kind correspondence with the open-minded editor of the *Living Church* of 1905-1906, U.S.A.

My thanks are hereby heartily given to Sir Henry H. Bemrose for the exceedingly generous way in which he has taken up the production of this volume with no expense whatever to myself. Though the subject seemed well worthy of presentation to the Christian Church, I saw no way of carrying out my wish until he intervened.

The Rev. John Booth, Vice-Principal of the Church Missionary Society's Cottayam College, most kindly supplied the best views reproduced herein, and I am greatly obliged to him. I must apologise to the Rev. F. N. Askwith, the Principal, my old friend, that I was not able to seek his aid for the better representation of Cottayam College, which has been such a boon to the Syrians—the only college of general education until recent days, for over forty years affiliated to the Madras University, and the first English high school ever founded in Malabar, certainly in Travancore and Cochin. It would take pages to enumerate its distinguished sons, and Mr. Askwith is the representative of a long line of able and beloved principals.

The editorial department of the Church Missionary Society have supplied the excellent photograph of the Baker Memorial High School, a new development of a venerable institution. I must apologise to the Principal, Miss Baker, for the liberty I take of using a photograph of some Syrian girls before I had her reply to my request for permission to insert it.

Archdeacon Caley has also kindly lent me some photographs, principally groups and portraits of Syrian Metrans and clergy.

I have used the photograph of my fellow-worker, Rev. K. M. Matthai, and his family, without asking a permission which I know he would not refuse.

For some of the facts relating to Mar Matthew Athanasius I am indebted to the deeply interesting history of the Church Missionary Society's work for the Syrian Church, which appeared in the *Malayala Mitram* (Friend of Malabar), a vernacular monthly, of which my old pupil and friend, Mr. John Chandy, the Superintendent of the Cottayam Mission Press, was editor, and to which he, himself of Syrian descent, contributed the history.

As I have not had the opportunity of submitting the following chapters to my friend, the Right Reverend Charles Hope Gill, D.D., Bishop in Travancore and Cochin, to whom I am honorary chaplain, it is but right to say that his lordship is in no way responsible for anything expressed therein.

It seems hardly necessary to say how grateful

I am to Mr. Eugene Stock (author of the famous *History of the Church Missionary Society*, and of many other books serviceable to the Church) for the ready way in which he agreed to my request to write a short preface. His kind words will supply a favouring breeze to fill the sails of my little venture, and waft it into the harbour of popular acceptance.

I commend this little volume to the blessing of God, and pray that it may help towards the building up of an Autonomous, Catholic, Reformed, and Evangelistic Church in the regions consecrated, as I believe, by the labours and blood of St. Thomas, the Apostle of His Blessed Son our Saviour Jesus Christ.

W. J. RICHARDS.

Lindfield, Sussex,
March 19*th*, 1908.

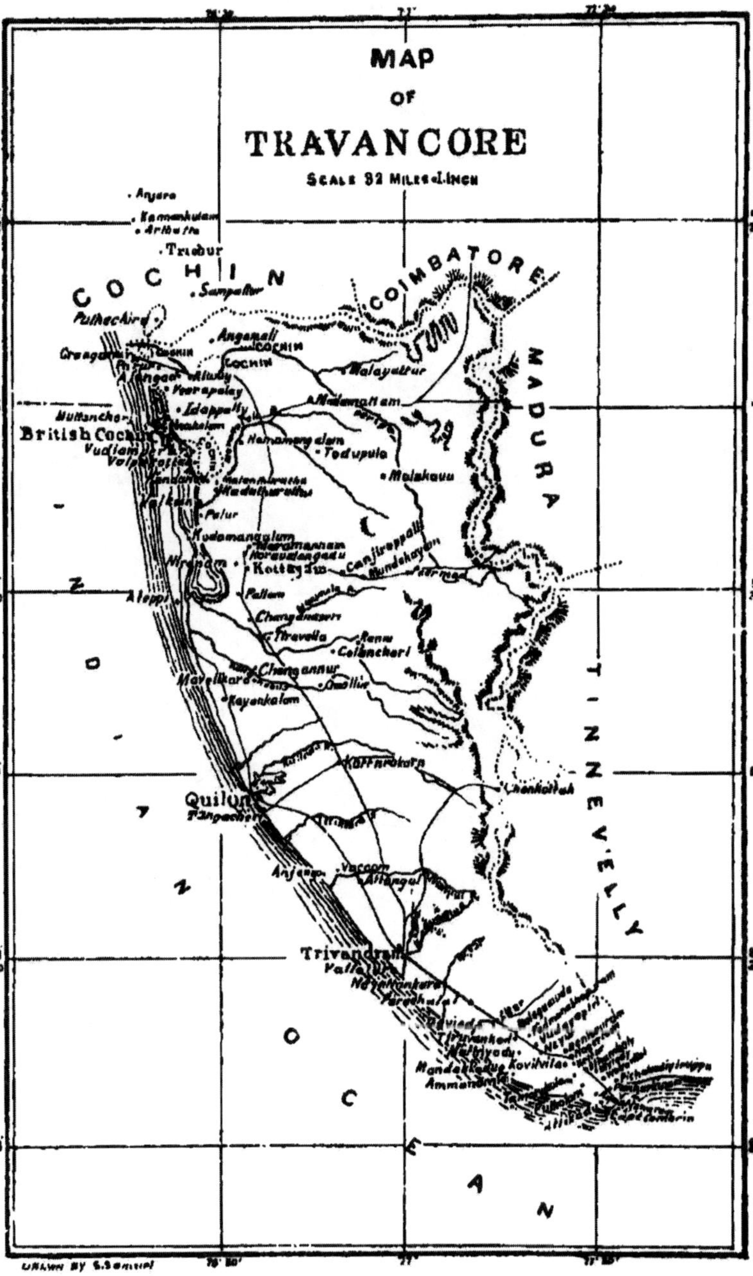

Mārāmannu, the centre of the Reformation, is on the north bank of the river, opposite Colancheri.

THE INDIAN CHRISTIANS OF ST. THOMAS IN THE NINETEENTH CENTURY

OR

One Hundred Years of God's Work in India for the Indian Christians of Malabar

✠

CHAPTER I.

THE CHRISTIANS AND THEIR EXTERNALS

THE Malabar Coast, on the west side of India, contains the Native Protected States of Travancore and Cochin. Cape Comorin, the most southern point of India, is in Travancore; the Cochin State is north of Travancore; and Calicut, the capital of British Malabar (whence "calico," the stuff and the name), is on the northern boundary of the Cochin State.

At Calicut the Portuguese admiral, Vasco da Gama, made his first landing on an Indian coast in 1498, five years after his discovery of the route from Western Europe to India by the Cape of Good Hope.

The Ancient Christians.—But, surely, the most striking discovery made by the daring Portuguese in that pagan land was the Christians of St. Thomas. The census of the two States in 1901 gives their number as 564,660, and in those far-away times they might have been a hundred thousand.

Their Various Names.—Sometimes they have been called the Christians of the Serra.[1] This arose from the fact of their living at the foot of the Ghauts, which rise to 9,000 feet high, and form the eastern boundary of Travancore and Cochin. These "mountains of God" bend their shielding arm, on the north, towards the Indian Ocean, which forms the western boundary; and so the two States are set in a position which has, so far, sheltered them from successful invasion. They are, since 1795 or so, allied to the British.

They are called St. Thomas Christians because they claim the Apostle Saint Thomas as their spiritual father. Because their Scriptures and their liturgies are in Syriac (which, by the way, was the language of our Blessed Saviour), or perhaps because they were reinforced from Syria in the ages gone by, they are called Syrian Christians. Sometimes, again, they are known as Nestorians; and since the year 1655, when they took the Jacobite Patriarch of Antioch as their head, they have been Jacobite Syrians, or, shortly, Jacobites. These names will be duly explained later on.

Their Physical Surroundings.—Travancore and Cochin are countries blest of the Creator. Beautiful with the ever-charming variety of hills and valleys,

---

[1] A Portuguese word, meaning mountains.

rivers and lakes, and a long stretch of sea coast, they are also endowed with a fertility begotten of the almost equatorial sun and the humid climate of the "zone of the greatest rain." The lakes, known locally as "backwaters," give a navigable length of a hundred and seventy miles parallel

CHERYA (LITTLE OR LATER) CHURCH, COTTAYAM.
Sketch showing chancel-roof, nave, and porch in the foreground.

with the sea. The whole territory is two hundred and fifty miles long, with an average width of about fifty miles. The rainfall is 150 to 250 inches.

Their Church Buildings.—Travancore and Cochin have been always admired by those who have been happy enough to visit them because of their lovely tropical foliage and picturesque scenery; and even to those who realise that India is a "heathen land," there is on this Malabar coast much to cheer their hearts. One of the objects oftenest seen is the Christian cross, a church, or a priest. The Syrians build their churches so that in profile one always sees the porch, the nave, and the chancel. The chancel has been described as a flattened tower, being square, and always higher than the nave, which, again, is always higher than the porch; and though built towards the East, the chancel lacks an east window. The western wall in modern days is adorned with plastered pillars and pinnacles, after the Portuguese fashion, and always shining white. The porch is sometimes fifty feet long, and is a place of general assembly and conversation. The roofs being red-tiled, the churches make a brilliant show against the dark green of the palm foliage amongst which they stand. There is a cross on every gable, and one rises from the centre of the four-roofed chancel tower, and often it is of wrought iron, in the Celtic shape. In high relief on the eastern and western walls of the church may be seen a cross supported by peacocks, and accompanied by various emblems, as wheels; and on churches that have at any time been under Roman influence, statues of saints, cut in the stone, and whitened, like the rest of the church, are found. Outside stands, usually, a grand granite cross, often twenty feet high, on a basement containing small cups cut in the stone to serve as lamps on days of saints, when it may be illuminated. A lofty wall of dark-red laterite, with a good coping, surrounds the churchyard; but there are—or rather were, when the missionaries first came in contact with the Syrians—no graves; the bones of the dead, after a year's burial in the porch, used to be taken up and thrown into a large dry well in a corner of the churchyard. A gate-house stands at the entrance of some churches, and there are often clergy-houses against the surrounding wall inside. At the west end of most churches, if not all, is a gallery, in which visiting bishops or clergy are expected to sleep, and there is a bed and a small detached wooden room for the chief guest. A brass lamp, in which a light is always kept, hangs from the roof in the nave before the sanctuary. A veil is drawn across the chancel arch, and in the sanctuary, which is approached by some steps, there is a stone altar, white plastered, with a wooden surface, breast high, and surmounted by a wooden cross. In some churches are two altars on the north and south sides of the nave against the east.

The priests are generally dressed in white cassocks, fastened at the side and shoulder, girt at the waist with a black band; and they wear a black silk or velvet cap. They are always full bearded. The bishop, or metran, wears a crimson satin robe, a golden girdle, and a sort of low mitre of black silk, ornamented with crosses of beaten gold, and having a flap, which hangs down the back of the neck. He also wears a pectoral cross, and at episcopal functions holds a pastoral staff, often of solid silver.

I have spoken of the crosses, and the churches,

and the priests to be seen inland, or along the lovely backwaters. Some of the latter are Roman Syrians; those for the most part on the sea-coast and the shores of the lagoons. The Portuguese,

A Snapshot (with apologies) of the "Reformed' Metropolitan TITUS MAR THOMA and his Suffragan standing in a native boat. Taken quite recently—1907. (It does not do them justice.)

three or four hundred years ago, were better able to coerce those who were on the water-ways than those living in the interior, "among the mountains," as they used to say.

Their Customs and Dress.—The Roman native clergy, always "shaven and shorn," generally dress most unsuitably for a moist, tropical climate, in shovel hats and black cassocks. The Jacobite priests, until the arrival of the Patriarch, 1875, wore white cassocks; now they wear mostly dark blue. The Reformers keep the ancient white robe, with girdle, as before mentioned. You can distinguish the people also by their outward appearance. All the men have the upper part of the body uncovered. The "Romans" wear round their necks the *scapular*, a small picture on white calico, about an inch square, of the Madonna and Child, or the Guardian Angel, etc.; and, on the reverse, a prayer, often in French, which they do not understand. One square hangs at the back and one in front. The non-Roman Syrians, living mostly on the east side of the lagoon, wear, as all the ordinary natives do, a white cotton cloth, reaching to the feet, and another thrown over the left shoulder. Their heads are bare, except when they are at work in the sun; otherwise they carry an umbrella, often the palm-leaf one of the country. The head is shaved, as well as the face, about once a month. (Hindus are distinguished by the sacred tuft, which in the Malayalam country is worn *in front* in a well-oiled top-knot. Moslems wear a white skull-cap.) The Syrians are often fair-complexioned. Syrian women dress in white, with a waist-cloth, which is doubled, and has a curious fan-shaped pleat behind. They wear a jacket also, and, when they appear in public, spread a large square of muslin over their heads, which hides the figure and gives them a graceful appearance. Sometimes it has a gold border. The feet in all cases are bare. Officials, teachers, and clerks don turbans or caps and cotton jackets during business hours. Very few men, I am glad to say, and no women, wear European clothes. The marriage badge is a tiny ornament of gold,

A GROUP OF SYRIAN GIRLS IN MISS BAKER'S SCHOOL, COTTAYAM.

with a cross in golden beads on it, and it hangs from a string (tied by the bridegroom) round the bride's neck. On occasions of ceremony, women and girls (well-to-do people always) deck themselves with necklaces of gold coins, Austrian or English, strung together with gold beads alternating, from which a small Maltese cross hangs on the breast.

Little children run about quite nude, except for a silver chain round the waist, with an ornament in front.

Baptismal Names.—Common Christian names are George (Gevarugisa, Varugisa, Varki, etc.), Thomas (Thoma, Thomman, Uṁman), John (Yohannan, Lonan), Luke (Lukōsa, Koshi), Cyril (Kuruwilla, Kuryan), Matthew (Matthai, Mātthan, Mātthu), Joseph (Yoseph, Ausep), Jacob (Chākko), Peter (Patros), Eso (Joshua or Esau), Alexander (Chandy), Abraham (Avira), Isaac (Itti, Ittak), Isaac-Abraham (Ittyera), and most of the Gospel names. Women are Mary (Mariam), Achi (?), Achambila (?), Sarah, Elizabeth (Eli), Anna, Eunice (Unichi), Rebecca (Akka), etc.

CHAPTER II.

ST. THOMAS—THE NESTORIANS—ROME—REVOLT

The History of the Malabar Christians.—According to their own account, these ancient Christians owe their existence to the Apostle St. Thomas, who they say preached the Gospel first on the Eastern or Coramandel Coast, near what is now Madras, and later on the Malabar Coast. They believe that he converted many Brahmans, ordained two presbyters or priests, built seven churches, and, returning to the east coast, was martyred.

Their Decadence.—When the clergy ordained by St. Thomas died, the Church fell into evil ways. Some of the converts, under the strain of persecution and persuasion, relapsed into Hinduism, and, according to the native account, their apostasy is connected with the revival in South India of the worship of Siva, brought about by a celebrated Hindu preacher named Mānika Vāchakar.

Their Reinforcement.—They were once more built up in the faith by the Nestorian Catholicos[1]

[1] Or Katholikos = Patriarch, a dignity given to five great bishops by the Early Church.

of Jerusalem, who sent Joseph, a bishop of Edessa, with priests and deacons, and seventy families, to revive their dying Christianity. The Syrians say

GRANITE SLAB,

About three feet high, with Pahlavi (ancient Persian) inscription, dating from the seventh century A.D. The cross is supposed to be surmounted by a dove. Inscription: "He that believes in the Messiah and God in the height and also in the Holy Ghost is in the grace of Him Who suffered the pain of the Cross." There is a facsimile slab at St. Thomas' Mount, Madras (see page 12).

this was in A.D. 345, but we know, from copper documents in their possession, and granted in the eighth century, that they received great privileges and position from the dominant ruler in Southern India at the latter date.

Connection with Persia.—The defective form of Christianity known as Nestorianism penetrated even into China about the same time, 735, and to this date must be ascribed the crosses and inscriptions in the ancient Persian (or Pahlavi) character found in Cottayam, and at St. Thomas' Mount, Madras, places five hundred miles apart. This language owns no inscription in India later than the eighth century. The church tradition among the St. Thomas Christians records the arrival on the Malabar Coast, from time to time, of bishops from Persia and Asia Minor, beginning with the year 825.

Contact with Europeans.—Our own King Alfred the Great, in fulfilment of a vow, sent a bishop to the tomb of St. Thomas in India more than a thousand years ago. (Of this more will be said hereafter.) Ser Marco Polo, the famous Venetian traveller, A.D. 1259, and John de Marignolli, a Minorite friar, 1346, describe their meeting with these Syrian Christians. The next name of note is that of Vasco da Gama, before mentioned, in the year 1498.

The Portuguese Protectors.—The astonishing meeting of Christian brethren in a heathen land so unexpectedly must have been equally pleasing to the Portuguese and to the St. Thomas Christians; the adventurers find allies where they expected enemies, the St. Thomas Christians, mighty protectors, Christians like themselves, in the face of the heathen and Muhammedans, from the latter of whom much was to be feared. It can easily be supposed that both Syrians and Portuguese would fall in love with one another at first sight, without any hypocrisy. Never, it seems to me, did anything appear more providential since Joseph's brethren went down into heathen Egypt and found in the chief official of that world-empire a loving brother.

Two Surprises for the Portuguese.—The pleasure of the European discoverers was soon to receive two shocks. These Indian Christians knew nothing of the Papal supremacy. Their Mother Church, that of Babylon, with their Patriarch living at Mosul, in Asia Minor, had never been subject to the Pope (or Patriarch) of Rome. The Council of Nicea, 325, had divided all bishoprics of the Church into five Patriarchates, of which old Rome was first, and governed the west, and the remainder were those of new Rome (or Constantinople), Alexandria, Antioch, and Jerusalem. The second surprise was that they were Nestorians, that is, followers of Nestorius, Patriarch of Constantinople, who was condemned by the General Council of Ephesus (431) for denying the One Personality of our Lord Jesus Christ. Nestorius held that Jesus was both God and Man, but asserted that the Deity came upon Him only at His Baptism; whereas the true faith is that Jesus was God even in the womb of His mother. It must soon have appeared to the Portuguese a most sacred duty to reunite these erring Christians to the faith of the Athanasian

Creed. Then, as the sixteenth century proceeded, and the revolt in Europe from unscriptural doctrines and from the Papal supremacy seemed permanent in England, France, Germany, Switzerland, and other European countries, what more fitting work for Roman Catholics than to bring this Eastern Church to the Catholic Faith, and to the feet of the Pope?

The intercourse marred by these differences had run a varied course for nearly a hundred years. By this time the Portuguese supremacy was attained in India. Goa, on the West Coast, sixteen degrees north, had become their capital, the seat of their Archbishop, and the headquarters of the terrible Inquisition. The Jesuit Order had been established in Europe, and was active in South India.

The Subjugation to the Pope of Rome.—Alexius de Menezes, the Archbishop of Goa, a Jesuit, and gifted with the characteristic astuteness and energy of that Order, determined to do the subjugating work. He claimed the Syrian Church as part of the patrimony of Rome, and summoned a Synod at Diamper (or Udiampērūr), near Cochin, to be held in 1599. This was by order of Pope Clement VIII., "to reduce them to the obedience of the Holy Roman Church, and purge out the heresies and false doctrines sown among them, and introduced by the schismatical prelates and Nestorian heretics that governed them under the obedience of the Patriarch of Babylon." [1]

---

[1] The words of the Bull (Geddes). *The History of the Church of Malabar*, 1694.

In order to ensure success, the Archbishop ordained so many new clergy from among the Syrians that they formed two-thirds of the one hundred and fifty-three clergy of the Synod, and, of course, carried all the decrees which he had brought, already written in his own hand-writing, to the Synod. As one would expect, their ancient Church views were condemned: they themselves convicted, sometimes mistakenly, of evil practices: and the Archbishop of Goa was accepted as the head of the Syrian Church under the Pope. Their Church Service books were altered to suit the Roman doctrines, invaluable manuscripts of theology and church history, etc., were burned, and after ten months of strenuous visiting and organizing the Archbishop returned to Goa. The Syrian Church in Malabar was thus brought under Rome, and continued its submission for half a century, with much ill-will on the part of the Syrians and their leading archdeacon. Great was the misery caused to these poor Indian Christians, and no less than three of their bishops, in or through the Inquisition at Goa, came to violent ends.

The Separation from the Roman Obedience.—In 1653, roused by the disappearance of one of these prelates, a Jacobite Patriarch from Antioch, styled Mar Ignatius (according to the Latin writers Jarri and Paolo, burned at Goa), the oppressed Christians assembled under their Archdeacon Thomas, and at the church cross of Mattanshêri, near Cochin, they swore that they would no longer obey the Portuguese bishops, and a large party, amounting by the census of 1901 to a quarter of a million, has until recent years obeyed the Jacobite Patriarch of Antioch, about 200,000 still doing so; the remainder being Reformed, under autonomous bishops.

MALABAR VILLAGE SCENE.

CHAPTER III.

More Changes—Alliance with English—Rupture

The change from Babylon to Antioch; from Nestorian to Jacobite.—When the Portuguese, in 1599, brought about the subjugation of the Nestorian or Syrian Church of Malabar, they took measures to render it lasting. Knowing that the Syrians looked to Babylon for metrans or bishops, they reasoned that if they could cut off the supply of bishops, the Syrians, being an episcopal Church, must perforce continue subject to Rome or cease to be episcopal. Therefore the Portuguese land and sea forces watched every way by which Patriarchs of Babylon or their deputies could reach South India. If any landed, the Portuguese compelled them to swear allegiance to the Pope, when they might possibly admit them to the country, but sometimes they shipped them to Europe or to Goa. The result was that no free Nestorian bishop could get into touch with the Syrians, and at length they were in great straits. However, in 1665, a Jacobite Patriarch of Jerusalem, Mar Gregorius, succeeded in effecting his entrance into Malabar, and was gladly received by those who would not be obedient to Rome. To make sure of a succession of Oriental bishops they also became Jacobites. Thus they adopted, unlikely though it was, the views which were most opposed to their own, namely, the belief that the Divine and Human Natures in our Lord were so united that there was but One Nature resulting, that is, the Godhead and Manhood mingled, to use their own phrase, "like wine and water."

Or Monophysite.—Hereby they are guilty of "confounding the Substance" (Essence, or Being, or Natures) of Christ. Hence they are called *Monophysites*, or those who hold one only Nature. *Jacobites* is another name applied to them, and is derived from a great Monophysite bishop of the sixth century, named Mar Jacob.[1] This change was made the more easily owing to the destruction of their Nestorian books at and after the Synod of 1599.

Mar Gregorius, the Syrian Patriarch of Jerusalem, who first introduced Monophysite doctrines into the Malabar Church, is stated by Paulinus a Roman friar about 1787, to have been distinguished by the following doctrines:—

1.—That the Pope and Nestorius were both heretics.

2.—That Antioch is the head and mother of the world.

3.—That Christ had one nature, the Divine.

4.—That the Holy Spirit proceeds only from the Father.

5.—That there is no purgatory.

---

[1] Gibbon's *Decline and Fall*, vol. iv., chap. xlvii. (II.).

As to the last article, it is not true of the present Jacobites. As to 3 and 4, information is given elsewhere.

In the direct contest with Rome the fight of the St. Thomas Christians was active, enduring, and long continued. The Syrians of that day were the best warriors in the country, and could put 30,000 brave soldiers in the field (*Christianity in Travancore*, Mackenzie, p. 63, n. 31). Once they necessitated the fortifying of Cochin by the Portuguese to resist possible attack. The fight, however, was one of moral force and spiritual opposition, and arms were seldom appealed to. For a long time, having no bishops, their ruling archdeacon, for several generations, endured, plotted, submitted, and rebelled, struggling bravely for their Church liberty, and supported by spirited laymen no less than by determined cattanars (priests).

The coming of the English.—Meanwhile the Dutch, 1663, had taken Malabar from the Portuguese, and they in their turn had to give way to the English in 1795. This put the Jacobites in a position of freedom. In the providence of God, the Marquis of Wellesley in 1806, when Governor-General of India, sent the Rev. Claudius Buchanan, D.D., Vice-Provost of the College of Fort William, Calcutta, to make researches among these ancient Christians. Dr. Buchanan was kindly received by the metran then in power. Right glad was the aged bishop to welcome a learned and liberal priest who owed no allegiance to the persecuting Church of Rome.

The English had just delivered Travancore and Cochin from the fangs of Tippoo Sultan, the Tiger of Mysore. The Metran described the state of the Syrians as that of a "declining Church." He welcomed the proposition of Dr. Buchanan that the clergy should translate the Scriptures from Syriac, a dead language to the laity, into Malayalam, the Indian language spoken by the Syrians of Malabar; and, said he, with eagerness, "I have already considered the subject, and have determined to superintend the work myself. . . . It is a work which will illuminate these dark regions, and God will give it His blessing." There was one Gospel already in the spoken language, namely, St. Matthew, but it was in manuscript only.

The Coming of the Church Missionary Society's Missionaries.—The Syrian Metran requested also that English clergy might be sent to help him and his people. This petition was backed up by Colonel Munro, the British Resident at the Courts of Travancore and Cochin. Ten years after, in 1816, his prayer was answered by the arrival of the Rev. Thomas Norton, followed by the Rev. Benjamin Bailey, the Rev. Joseph Fenn, and the Rev. Henry Baker, missionaries sent by the Church Missionary Society with instructions not to proselytize from the ancient Church, but to co-operate with the Syrian bishops and clergy in every possible way, and to aim at bringing about a reformation within the Church both of doctrines and of morals, and, if possible, a friendly union of Churches.

The hopes of the Church Missionary Society.— It will be interesting to quote here some of the "instructions" of the parent committee of the Church Missionary Society to the first missionaries. For instance, on 28th October, 1817, when the Rev. Joseph Fenn and Rev. Henry Baker were leaving for Travancore, they were addressed as follows:—

> "Messrs. Norton and Bailey are situated near the Syrians, and are on the most friendly terms with the bishop and clergy, by whom they have been gladly welcomed. . . . It was the opinion of Dr. Buchanan that the Church of England could not as a National Church employ her influence to greater advantage than in restoring and building up the ruins of the Syrian Communion in Antioch, in Mesopotamia, and in India. When this was accomplished, he considered that those countries would supply missionaries for the extension of the Christian faith among the Mohammedans and Pagans. Our design in sending you among the Syrian Christians is that you should by every suitable means in your power promote these objects in India."

We see from this extract the aim of the Church Missionary Society, which was nothing different from that of the Archbishop of Canterbury's Mission to the Nestorian Christians in Asia Minor at the present time. Perhaps the Church Mission had the more definite object in seeking to bring about an internal reformation of the ancient Church in India; but there was no idea of proselytizing. Then the committee went on to set forth the Gospel doctrines which the missionaries were to preach, namely, the ruin of man by sin, and the complete redemption by Jesus Christ promised to the believer, and the need of the sanctifying help of the Holy Ghost. The following words of wisdom are worthy of being written in letters of gold:—

"We recommend you to avoid discussions and disputings on the mysterious questions concerning the Nature of Christ, which first divided and afterwards ruined the Churches of the East, and rather to lead their minds to the plain and important truths of the Gospel. . . . We think with Dr. Buchanan that the revival of the Syrian Church will be the means of supplying efficient missionaries for surrounding Mohammedan and heathen countries."

The Doctrines of the Syrians of Malabar.—Since 1665 they had been Jacobite Syrians, yielding their allegiance, as we have seen, to the Jacobite Patriarch of Antioch. As a Church, they hold the Creed of Constantinople, given in our Communion Service, and called the "*Nicene Creed.*" This was the belief of the Catholic Church before the Nestorian and Jacobite errors began. In common, however, with the whole Eastern Church, they say it thus: "I believe in the Holy Ghost . . . proceeding from the Father," omitting "*and the Son,*" which in Latin is "*Filioque,*" and hence called "the *Filioque* clause." But as they do not deny that the Holy Spirit "receiveth" from the Son, they really are, on this article of faith, as orthodox as the Churches of England and Rome. Like the Church of Rome (perhaps from the Church of Rome) they had acquired those doctrines which we threw off at the Reformation: "Purgatory . . . worshipping and adoration of images and relics, and also invocation of saints." In one respect they were "more noble" than the Roman

Church, for they did honour to the Word of God, and welcomed it in the vernacular. They hold the threefold orders of bishops, priests, and deacons. They gave the wine-cup to the laity by dipping the wafer into it. Some of their pictures are said to have represented the Father, though in former times they refused to worship images.[1]

The Evil Practices of the Syrians of Malabar.—We are thinking of the years 1817 to 1837, when the missionaries had begun to work among them. Their chief errors, we may charitably say, were the result of ignorance of the Scriptures, and of mingling among the heathen. A popular image, the recipient of many offerings, was one of "St. George slaying the Dragon." Offerings to evil spirits were common. Superstitious purifications of women, and feasts for the repose of the soul after death, made on the fortieth day, were practised. Owing to Roman influence, the marriage of the clergy had been dropped. Church brawls were frequent. During festivals men and women slept at night in the churches. The *Kurubāna*, or Eucharist, was celebrated for money; sometimes for the dead, and sometimes that salaries might be obtained, or other earthly benefits. Ordeals, as practised by the heathen, were followed.

When we would picture the darkness of what their Metran described as the "declining Church" of St. Thomas in the days before Buchanan and the missionaries appeared upon the scene, we must

---

1 See Appendix for details.

imagine the state of ignorance where there is no preaching of God's Word, no version of the Scriptures for the people to read, non-preaching clergy, and a Church barely escaped from the direst persecution and still surrounded by dense, dark Romanism. Reckon, too, the fearful atmosphere of heathenism where it has had its own way, and has added to the ordinary chains of caste the peculiar and galling fetters of atmospheric pollution, and, what has been not unjustly described as polyandry, the unnatural sort of marriage which curses the Travancore royal family.

The Missionaries' Method of Work for the "Syrians."—The Rev. Joseph Fenn, writing after his arrival in Travancore, reports as follows to the Home Committee: "Mr. Bailey has secured, to a degree beyond what could have been expected, the confidence and esteem of the Syrian clergy and people. This has been no easy matter. Their jealousy of interference, and, above all, the licentious manners of the clergy, have concurred to render his situation one of peculiar delicacy and difficulty. . . . Many will raise every obstacle in their power to the adoption of measures to restrain their corrupt manners." Speaking generally of the people, he says: "They are greatly superior in point of moral principle and feeling to their neighbours, and instances of dishonesty are rare among them." He also commends their "fortitude and patience for suffering." Under another head he thinks it would be good for the missionaries to have a chapel for their own worship, remarking "not that we wish to impose any of our ceremonies upon them, much less to identify them with the English Church, but a model is necessary for them in this attempt at reformation. . . . Independently, then, of the Sunday service, we think it will be productive of advantage to observe all the festivals and fasts of our Church, and the weekly and occasional services."

The Rev. Thomas Norton, the first missionary, was stationed at Alleppey, the chief seaport of Travancore, and worked on the translation of the Bible, and preached to the heathen. The other three lived at Cottayam, eighteen miles away, and across the backwater. Mr. Bailey was the chief translator of the Scriptures; the four Gospels had been printed and published at Bombay in 1811, through the aid of Claudius Buchanan, and at the cost of the Bible Society. The translation was, for its time, a wonderful thing, the work of the Syrian clergy themselves; but the book produced was a big quarto volume, the language was unidiomatic, and the type very clumsy. Still it must have been a great blessing to the Malabar Syrians. Mr. Fenn taught the deacons in a college established at Cottayam by the British Resident. Mr. Baker's work was the establishing of village schools and itinerating among the Syrians. The missionaries were very careful not to make proselytes; in fact, this was the chief article of the committee's instructions to them. All their doings were with the approval of the Syrian Metran, and even their English children were baptized in the Syrian churches, for they had none of their own. They preached at church services and on public occasions, and went on trying to leaven the ancient Church with a perception of the beauties of primitive doctrine and reformed practices. Apparently the only effort that was quite successful was that for the reintroduction of marriage among the clergy, and this was brought about by the offer on the part of the British Resident of special dowries to the first women who would accept priests as husbands. The women were at this time superstitiously afraid to marry priests; but there is a particular and honourable name in use for a priest's wife—namely, Baskiāma (Syriac), a witness to their ancient customs. Four claimed the four hundred rupees offered, and when others saw the happiness of the first clerical marriages they followed the example, and the custom has gone on ever since.

Discontent and Suspicions.—The work of the missionaries, and of those who came out from England to help or succeed them, was patiently continued for twenty years. So close was the connection that certain properties were held in common between the Metran and the missionaries, under carefully defined rules, for the purpose of the work. Such was the Cottayam College and its endowments. But the favouring Metran passed away, and his successors were less friendly. Many of the priests became opposed to reform. New missionaries were perhaps too precipitate and unreasonably dissatisfied with the results attained by the patient labours of the older missionaries.

The Rupture.—Anyhow, it was found necessary for the missionaries to separate from the Syrians, and turn to the heathen, for the ancient Christians, in 1835, held a council at Mavelikara, a large Syrian town, and were compelled by the Metran to take an oath that they would "have no intercourse whatever with the Church missionaries," and the young clergy were prohibited from attending the college, the Metran altogether withdrawing his permission and support from the missionaries. To complete the separation, which, on the part of the missionaries, took place in 1837, the Indian Government, in 1840, sanctioned an arbitration committee, which divided the property hitherto jointly held, the Church Missionary Society and the Metran getting the properties which severally were theirs, or committed to them as trustees for the benefit of the Syrians.

CHAPTER IV.

THE REMNANT—A WYCLIF—THE REFORMATION

The Unexpected Result.—Can anything be conceived more saddening for the Church Missionaries and the Home Society? Their work for the Syrians was closed, but not one of the clergy seemed to have come forward as a hearty reformer. And the people, too, seemed as if they "loved to have it so." It was like the reception of our Lord and His Apostles at the hands of the Jewish Church. But some of the Syrians had imbibed a love for the missionaries. They valued the doctrines which they taught, and the expositions of the Holy Scriptures, and the use of prayers in the vernacular. When, therefore, the missionaries went forth to the heathen, some hundreds of the Syrians went with them, and supplied the men necessary for catechists, schoolmasters, and clerks.

A Martyr.—It is hard now to realise the bitterness of the immense majority of the Syrians who remained and sympathised with the Metran. The following, taken from Bagster's *The Bible of Every Land*, speaks volumes:—

"Some years ago a Syrian named Curiathu was reclaimed from a most sinful course of life by a study of the Gospels, a copy of which he had received from Rev. J. Ridsdale. He became quite another man, abandoned his worldly, covetous, and self-seeking views, and began to preach the Gospel of our Lord Jesus Christ with a self-denial, zeal, and boldness seldom to be witnessed. He was quite careless of worldly emoluments, and many times refused pecuniary assistance, travelling penniless, and contented to live on casual alms. How much he suffered for Christ cannot be known, for he never revealed such matters. He was preaching in Kunnankulam bazaar when an opposer of the truth, a Syrian, went home for a knife, and stabbed Curiathu through the heart. With a prayer to God not to lay this sin to the charge of the murderer, Curiathu immediately fell lifeless."

THE BAZAAR, KUNNANKULAM, IN NATIVE COCHIN.
Showing Native Shops (see above).

A Syrian Wyclif.—What wonder if the early Church Missionaries were inclined to despair of the Syrian Church? But, whether they knew it or not, they had begun, even for the ancient Church, a good work.

Among the professors, or Malpâns, in the Cottayam College was the pious Kattanar, or priest,

Abraham, whose comfortable home was south-east of Cottayam, on the high banks of the lovely river Rânni. Malpân Abraham sympathized with the spiritual aims of the missionaries, and when, on the breaking up of the coalition between the missionaries and the Syrian Metran, he returned to his home and parish of Mārāmannu he began to carry out the principles which lie at the very root of all religious reform by conducting the worship of God and preaching in a tongue understood of the people. Among other things insisted upon by Malpân Abraham, and introduced so far as his influence went, certainly in his own parish, were the restoration of Holy Communion in both kinds, and communicating the people during service. He protested against masses for the dead and masses performed for money (within recent years a heathen paid a fee to have the Eucharistic Sacrament celebrated to procure him an appointment). Prayers to the saints he declared to be useless. In fact, he was the Wyclif of the Syrian Church in Malabar.

The Work amongst the Heathen.—Meanwhile missionary work went on apace among the worshippers of the foul deities of Hinduism (the high castes) and among the down-trodden and degraded devil-worshippers (or low castes) of the country—notably, the Rev. Joseph Peet's work among the Chogans or palm tree cultivators of Mavelikara and the southern part; the Rev. Henry Baker (Junior's) work among the hill-men east of Cottayam; and that of the Rev. John

Hawksworth at Mallapalli and Tiruwella for the "slaves," the "polluting" Pulayans, in the rice-fields. The states of Travancore and Cochin are "mad upon their idols." The country is a survival of "old" India, having never been overrun by Moslem invaders. The Syrian Church had paid a very high price for Hindu toleration. She gave up the power to witness for her Lord, she gathered not with Him, and so she barely lived as a caste among the castes; not as a Christian Church—a lamp set on a lamp-stand, but as a light hidden under a bushel—salt that had lost its saltness. The Jacobite Syrians, to whom the missionaries came, had indeed passed by the heathen on the other side. In those old days the bell of Mavelikara church was never rung for fear of doing a discourtesy to the Goddess of Blood in the temple hard by! Now they saw converts, if but a few, from influential castes, and multitudes from among the others, all over the low country. In 1848 work began among the hill-men, but the lowest depth was reached when, in 1854, the Pulayans (or polluters)—down-trodden slaves, bought and sold like cattle—were sought out by the Church Missionary Society's missionaries, pastors, and catechists.

The Syrians desire the Gospel.—The Syrians saw congregations being formed, stone churches built, native clergy ordained, the latter mostly if not altogether from the Syrians who joined the missionaries. Then the Syrians who had rejected the truth began to desire the advantages which fell to those whom they had allowed to remain idolaters and demon-worshippers. They desired, in fact, to be fed with the bread which the poor "slaves" had in such plenty. One after another rose up who spoke of these things, and cultivated friendly relations with Church Missionary Society native clergy and missionaries.

How Reform Grew.—Boys, of whom hundreds were educated in Cottayam College, the chief school of the Mission, were led to love the Gospel of the Blessed God. The message was taught in all the vernacular schools; even the Maharajah appointed a Christian to teach the Gospel in his college where Syrian youths came to learn. Colporteurs and catechists spread the printed Word all over the country. Thus it came to pass that some Syrian clergy began to preach to the people in Malayalam, and the Scriptures were read in Syrian homes and groups of families. Girls were taught in the Missionary boarding-schools. "English" being a paying article, and University degrees valuable, some Syrian students went to the Free Church College, Madras, and the Rajah's colleges at Trevandrum, the capital of Travancore, and at Ernakulam, the capital of Native Cochin. Everywhere they came in contact with reformed Christianity, and were inspired with admiration for its life and liberty.

No Proselytism.—In all my thirty-five years' experience of Malabar, I do not remember one Syrian choosing to become a Roman Catholic, nor proselytism, either by the Church Missionary

A SIDE VIEW OF THE C.M.S. COLLEGE HALL, COTTAYAM.

The open space is common, and is outside the "College compound" or premises. The tall and feathery trees are Australian Casuarinas.

D

Society, the London Missionary Society, or the Free Kirk, Madras; not to speak of the Basel Evangelical Mission in Malabar, with which some of the Syrians came in contact. I do not mean to say that since 1837 no Syrians have become

THE BAKER MEMORIAL HIGH SCHOOL FOR GIRLS, COTTAYAM.

Founded to commemorate three generations of ladies who worked for the elevation of Syrian and other Malayalam girls: Mrs. Baker (senior), 1818; Mrs. Henry Baker, 1843; and Miss Mary Frances Baker to 1888.

Anglicans. It must be that eventualities of this kind should occur, especially when marriages take place between members of the different churches; but what I would have remembered is that whenever a Syrian individual or family desired to join the

Church Missionary Society—the only Anglican society at work in Travancore—the invariable advice of the Church missionaries has been: "Keep to your own Church, and share any fresh light you have received, any new knowledge of God, or of peace through Christ, which you have gained, with your own people." In this way the desire for reformation spread among the Syrians, until a strong Reform Movement was seen to rise and develop in many quarters.

CHAPTER V.

A REFORMING METROPOLITAN—AN EXCOMMUNICATING PATRIARCH

The Reformation finds a Bishop as Leader.—When the missionaries first came to the aid of the St. Thomas Christians it was at the request of a Syrian Bishop, and when the friendly relations were severed it was by the hostile action of another Bishop; and it is quite in keeping with all the history of the Syrian Church that the Reformation should be made or marred by a Bishop.

Mar Athanasius.—The Reforming movement on the part of the Syrian clergy had begun, we saw, with the beginning of the work among the heathen. It was carried on during the episcopate of Mar Athanasius. The story demands that we should give a sketch of his life.

We have mentioned the former professor at the old college, who became the Wyclif of Malabar. He had two pupils (born in 1818), and very promising as students.

George Matthan.—A Syrian becomes the first Anglican Minister.—One was his nephew, Matthew, and the other a certain George Matthan. When the split took place between the missionaries and the new Metran, both Matthew and George Matthan were excommunicated by their Bishop, and, as it was only on account of their sympathy with the missionaries, the latter took them up and sent them to the Church Missionary Society's Institution at Madras to complete their education for the ministry.

Their careers illustrate the way it sometimes pleases the Divine Head of the Church to carry out His own purposes. George Matthan, despairing of any reformation, or moved with pity for the heathen, and partly, perhaps, for his own spiritual good, cast in his lot with the missionaries, and was eventually ordained the first Malayalam clergyman of the Anglican Church, and, after a life of much usefulness and fruitbearing, entered into rest in the year 1870, leaving behind him some valuable literary works.

Deacon Matthew's Career.—Deacon Matthew committed a breach of rules by using translations ("cribs") in his preparation of work, and had to leave the Madras Institution.

It is not my purpose to dwell upon the various details of his adventurous career, it must for the present suffice to say that he went to Antioch, in Syria, with letters from his people to the Jacobite Patriarch, who made him full priest, and then consecrated him Metran, and sent him back to Malabar in the year 1843 to rule over the Syrian Church.

"I will yet live to pluck out the weeds by the roots, and reduce our Church to its pristine purity and simplicity of faith," were the inspiring words which he uttered in the teeth of the excommunication under which he had gone to Syria; and now he had returned with the necessary power, and singularly fitted for so high a work, had he been a consistently good man. He had received a capital English education, and was a competent Syriac scholar, and while in Antioch had acquired a knowledge of Arabic. He also knew the Truth. But, alas! his actions as Bishop belied his fine words.

An Ungodly Metran.—Contrary to the advice of his uncle, the reforming Malpan Abraham, he went to law against the Metran already in power; he opposed reform in every possible way, and his life was marked by so much ungodliness that the aged Reformer, when on his death-bed in 1845, refused the Eucharist at such unholy hands, preferring the help of humbler but better priests, and so Malpan Abraham, the father of the Syrian Reformation, fell asleep in Jesus at the early age of fifty-one, his end saddened by the failure of many hopes.

The Reformation, however, was not dead, and the light of the Gospel was held forth by worthy Kattanars or priests who succeeded him at Mārāmannu and in its neighbourhood.

(The present reforming Metran, Titus Mar Thoma, and his two predecessors, are of the same family.)

Recognized as Metropolitan.—His nephew, known henceforth as Mar Athanasius Matthew, persevered in his litigation until, in 1857, recognized as head of the Syrian Church in Travancore and Cochin by the British Resident and the native princes, he could rule his diocese without a rival.

His aim now was directed towards conciliation, and there was for several years small hope of reformation in his own life or in the practices of his Church.

His Repentance.—Eventually, however, he gave up all his evil doings, moved to repentance, I have heard, by the godly counsels and warnings of a brother Bishop, Dr. Milman, the Metropolitan of all India, in about 1870, or a little earlier.

I can bear testimony—as from 1871 until 1877, when he died, we were neighbours in Cottayam—that his latter years were exemplary, and he did set himself to reform the Church, but his efforts were marred by his too astute attempts to please both the Reformers and their enemies. He would say the prayers in Syriac, when such was the practice of the Kattanars whose churches he might happen to be visiting, although in his own chapel and among the growing number of Reformers he preferred the vernacular.

His Suffragan and Successor.—During his lifetime he consecrated to be his Suffragan a cousin, Mar Thomas Athanasius, who, on his succeeding to the episcopal throne as Metropolitan in 1877, was honoured and encouraged by the loyalty of the reforming clergy and laity among his people.

Rival Parties.—Then there was a Metran who led those opposed to reformation. He too had been consecrated by the Jacobite Patriarch, and took the name of Mar Dionysius V. Thus the Syrian Church—that is, the non-Roman section—was seen with two parties struggling for the mastery and

Most Rev. Mar Dionysius V.

Jacobite Metropolitan. Consecrated 1865.

for the possession of the churches, their properties, and endowments. The contest had come to a head in 1875, when the Jacobite Patriarch of Antioch actually visited Travancore at the request of the non-Reformers, and set on foot lawsuits in the Hindu courts to deprive Mar Athanasius Matthew of any authority he had received from the former Patriarch, or from the British Resident and the Native Governments; and when the Patriarch once more returned to Antioch, he left behind him *seven* Bishops, of whom he had consecrated six, to continue the struggle and reduce the Syrian Church completely to his obedience. He also excommunicated the Reforming Metran.

The factions were known among themselves as the "Patriarch's Party" and the "Metran's." The struggle narrowed itself to the question: Shall the Church remain under the Patriarch of Antioch and unreformed, or shall it break loose and have no foreign head? Thus things went on to a state of active warfare. It was like living in England in the sixteenth century. Parishes were divided among themselves, one part of the parish clergy being for and another against reformation. Families, too, were rent asunder, and it was once more seen what our Lord meant when He said that He came not to send peace, but a sword.

Death and Pastoral of Mar Athanasius Matthew.—In 1877 the Reforming Metran, Mar Athanasius Matthew, as we have said above, died. He was ill for some months, suffering much from the poisonous effects of a rat's bite. Shortly before his

RIVER NEAR COTTAYAM.

Coco-nut palms. Boats, and men poling with long bamboos.

death he addressed the following Pastoral, in Malayalam, to his flock, sending a copy to each church :—

To the Vicar, Curates, Churchwardens, and other members of the —— Church.

"Grace, peace, and all blessing from God the Father and the Lord Jesus Christ be with you all.

"BELOVED CHILDREN,—We thank our God that He chose, called, and appointed us, who are weak and sinful, to be your Bishop and spiritually to govern you, whom our Lord Jesus the Messiah has redeemed with His own most precious blood, and who are the people of His pasture and the sheep of His hand.

"The days of the years of our pilgrimage are sixty years; and now God having put it into our thoughts to consider that the time and season of our parting with this earthly tabernacle, and departing to our Heavenly Father are fast approaching, we, from our couch of sickness, write this as our final letter to you, and thereby bid you farewell before this our body, which is the earthly tabernacle, breaks up. We commit our spirit into the Almighty hands of the Lord Messiah, our Saviour, Who laid down His life for His sheep, and we put our full trust in Him that He will take us into the land of those who have gained victory, and that He will give us an inheritance in the heavenly Jerusalem that we may sing praises with those who are above in glory.

"Beloved, you have fully known the tenour of the doctrines which we, who are weak and sinful, from the time of our entering upon the episcopacy down to this present day have preached and expounded to you. That there is nothing in them which is strange or our own can be clearly discovered by every one who would compare them with the pure word of God, which maketh wise the simple and enlighteneth the eyes, and which is more to be desired than gold, and to those who taste it is 'sweeter also than honey and the honeycomb.' Our children in the Lord, we exhort you again to stand firm on the true rock that has been preached to you so that you neither forsake the path of truth nor be deluded by Satan, and, that you may be enabled for it, put your entire trust in the grace of God. In the name of the Lord we ask your forgiveness if we have offended any of you either by word, deed, or letter. Dear Children, we remind you always to remember the words of the Bible, that the days of man are as grass and as the flowers of the field. Where are the mighty of the world? Where are the monarchs of the earth and its wise men? All have passed away according to their days and generations. Therefore we advise and admonish you that believing in the Lord Messiah, who died for our sins and rose again for our justification, and Who by His resurrection has conquered the world and the devil, and has taken away sin, you should resist those enemies, the world, the flesh, and the devil, and heartily yield your souls and bodies with all your members wholly for His glory and service. This may be our farewell sermon and final counsel to you. May the Lord the Messiah, Who is King of Kings and Lord of Lords, and to Whom only belongeth power, majesty, and glory, and Who is the Lion of the tribe of Judah, and the Bridegroom of Holy Zion, vouchsafe to grant you the spirit of His adoption, and keep you safe under His holy keeping that ye may also stand with us on His right hand in the great day of His manifestation when He shall appear with the ten thousands of His Holy Angels.

"In conclusion we beg of you to offer prayer for us to God without ceasing, that we may bear patiently the pains, trials, and anxieties that afflict us on our bed of sickness; that the needful comfort, peace, and strength may be granted to us, and that our soul may be kept from the wiles and snares of Satan until the moment of our last breath; and also that the remaining sanctification may be perfected in us by His Holy Spirit.

"Glory be to the Father, the Son, and Holy Ghost, the Triune God; and all His blessings and graces be with you all."

Mārāmannu Church, 10*th July*, 1877.

CHAPTER VI.

THE REFORMERS WIN TRUTH AND LOSE LAWSUITS

A Circular of the Reformers.—From the following ciicular, which I have translated out of the Malayalam original, we see the spirit of the Reformers when their beloved and indomitable Metropolitan was taken from them. We should also notice that they distinctly separate themselves from the errors of the Nestorians and Jacobites, thus associating themselves with Catholics holding the decrees of the four General Church Councils.

" The Holy Church of the Apostle St. Thomas in Malabar to all the brethren in the Malabar Diocese Greeting.

" DEARLY BELOVED.—The many defects in things religious and temporal that have happened to our ancient Church, which in point of age is inferior to no Church in other lands, can be easily perceived, and are known to all the spiritually and scripturally enlightened. Now although through the preaching of the Word of God at the present time Scriptural knowledge, the fear of God, and kindred things are more or less gaining ground in all our parishes, yet owing to the anti-scriptural teaching and superstitious practices brought in by the Nestorians, the Portuguese and the Jacobites, by which many are still fettered, the ministry of the Church are in the highest degree bound to toil that these evils may be uprooted, and that the Church may be established in the truth. As long as fields lie fallow it is impossible to do them much harm, although the owners be idle, but when once the soil is prepared and the seed sown, worms may destroy it, and blight may ruin the springing corn, yet all the time lookers-on may not know whence these evils arise. So while our Church lay unreformed there was no need on the part of Satan and his evil spirits to trouble it, though for the most part we were slack, but now that we have begun to reform, enemies from all parts hasten to destroy the Church. From one quarter come a party with superstitious hypocrisies and unscriptural traditions, and from an opposite quarter one wearing a pious garb, but really opposed to true religion; and, again, another party, not merely averse from the truth of the Bible, but aiming to overthrow it by unscriptural interpretations, revelations,[1] and dogmas, lying in ambush with full intent to destroy our Church. Again, the Jacobites may be seen ready to annihilate the ancient independence belonging to this our Church and its episcopate; and as members of our Church in former times were subjugated by the Nestorians and the Portuguese, so we see some to-day seduced to yield to Antioch. Accordingly our diocesans, the late Most Reverend Mar Athanasius Metropolitan and the Most Reverend Mar Thomas Athanasius, have urged upon our community the importance of having a godly Church Council to establish the true creed and the old independence of our Church and its bishops. It is the principal and most essential duty of the ministers of the Church to strengthen the true faith, to reform the Church, and to labour for its increase, and to bind the body together by the bond of love, so that they themselves may grow, and train you also in the fear of the Lord. The undersigned Committee therefore, full of zeal herein, have decided to form a godly Church Council, and have been deliberating in various churches on things pertaining to reformation, as at Tiruvilla in 1876, Mārāmannu in 1877, etc., etc. In the council held this day in Ayrur church we decided on this circular, and as members of this Committee humbly desiring your welfare we beg to address you. We well know that there are many earnest people, both clergy and laity, eager to join such a council, and who with sighing and

---

1 This is a reference to the "*Six Years Party*" which arose through the preaching of an ex-Brahman who was an Anglican pastor, and with his six brothers claimed to have had in 1875 a series of revelations from the Lord Jesus that He would return to judge the world in 1881. Some thousands of the Syrians were affected by it.

Reformed Metropolitan, with Kattarazand Deacons.

The Reformers keep to the ancient white cassock.

tears pray for the welfare of the Church. It is therefore needful that those who are fully minded to give their counsels herein, and who would bind themselves to all resolutions agreed upon touching the reformation and elevation of our Church should write signifying their names. Clergy and laymen are alike eligible. Six months after the receipt of this notice an important council will be summoned. In replying please send name, parish, etc., to Rev. K. M. Joseph, Priest of Chenganur, one of our clergy. The President of the Committee is the Right Rev. Mar Thomas Athanasius, Metropolitan.

"The following is a summary of things to be deliberated about the reformation of our Church:—The abolishing of traditions and practices founded on hypocrisy and superstition, prayers to the saints, intercessions for the dead, ceremonies contrary to the Scriptures. Then, decrees in accordance with Holy Writ, and conformable to our ancient Church customs, and for the establishing of the true Faith, have to be passed.

"May all the graces and blessings of God be in the councils of His humble servants.

"In the year of Christ, 1878 (28th of Taurus, Malayalam year 1053)."

(Here follow the names of nineteen consenting priests, one being a Malpan or Professor of Syriac and Theology, one the present reforming Metropolitan, and a couple of Vicars.)

The consistent non-interference of the Missionaries.—The traditional practice of the Church Missionary Society's Missionaries towards the Syrians as to parties may be seen from the following experience of my own. In 1874 I was in my house in Cottayam when a deacon, a youth of about eighteen, learning in the Syrian college, came to see me, and brought for my inspection a letter of the Syrian Patriarch of Antioch deposing the then reforming Metran Mar Athanasius with whom I was very friendly. To my mind this deacon was guilty of disloyalty to his Bishop, and I felt it my duty to show him to the door. The same evening I met the Rev. J. M. Speechly, afterwards our first Bishop, and told him the story. He laughed heartily at me, and said: "This is not the policy we should follow. You are misled by Mr. ——. We must be friendly with all the Syrians, and neutral as to their parties."

Some time before this, and while I was vice-principal of the Cottayam College (our English school, then under the Rev. J. H. Bishop), it fell to my lot to prepare the English-speaking candidates for confirmation. This was intended only for Anglicans. Some Syrian lads, however, being wishful to receive the Holy Communion in our out-station churches near their homes, begged to be presented for confirmation. It should be remembered that for the most part the Syrian priests at that time would only celebrate the Eucharist in Syriac, a dead language to those boys. I asked permission of Bishop Gell, then Bishop of Madras, our Diocesan at the time, to present them. The Bishop, however, declined, unless they had leave from their own Metran (bishop), to whom I at once applied and received his kind sanction. I mention this incident because it has been made by the Jacobites the ground of an accusation against me of proselytizing. The charge is false, because the very persons who made it, though confirmed, never became Anglicans, and knew that they were not expected to do so. It was more than thirty years ago, and the practice of presenting Syrians for Confirmation was never allowed by Bishop Speechly nor his successors, as they felt it would only lead to confusion.

The Bases of the Lawsuits.—The Decisions of the Courts.—We have before mentioned that the Jacobite Patriarch, when he visited Travancore in 1875, instituted lawsuits for the purpose of deposing the Reforming Metropolitan from power, and for dispossessing his party of the churches and their endowments. The contention of the Jacobites was that the Syrian Church of Malabar had always been under the jurisdiction of the Patriarch of Antioch, and that the Church was always Jacobite, and that no consecration of a Bishop (Metran) could lawfully take place without the authority of the Jacobite Patriarch.

The Reformers claimed that the Church had ever been autonomous, and altogether independent of Antioch. They admitted that at certain crises in the history of their Church, other Churches, as the Nestorians and the Monophysites, had kindly continued their episcopal ordinations; but they denied that such kindly help gave any right either to Nestorians or others to exercise permanent authority over them.

No doubt the Indian (and Hindu) judges, who decided in favour of the Patriarch's party, were influenced by the fact that for two hundred and twenty years the whole Church had submitted to the rule of the Jacobite Patriarchs of Antioch.

In each of the great cases of 1889 and 1901, the

single European judge entered a protest against the decision of the Hindu judges.

The lawsuits went on for over thirty years, and in the long run it was shown that neither in doctrines nor obedience to Antioch were the Reformers *Jacobites*, and they equally disown the mediæval doctrines gathered by contact with the Church of Rome.

It is interesting to know that after Mar Titus Thoma succeeded to the episcopal throne of St. Thomas the Apostle in 1894 he was greatly encouraged by a kind and sympathetic letter from the Archbishop of Canterbury, Dr. Benson. The first (Dr. John Martindale Speechly) bishop of the Anglican Church in Travancore and Cochin told me of this.

CHAPTER VII.

THE JACOBITES—THE REFORMERS AT LIBERTY—SOME ROMANS

The present condition of the (non-Roman) Syrians.—As shown by the census of 1901, the Jacobites and the Reformers together amount to two hundred and fifty-five thousand, and if we include their brethren under the Bishop of Anyura, reckoned at fourteen thousand, who are called Nasranis,[1] and who live in British Malabar, they number two hundred and seventy thousand. Three-fourths of these are Jacobites — that is, claiming the Monophysite Patriarch as their head. In India their ecclesiastical head is the Most Rev. Mar Dionysius V., who is assisted by two Metrans, all that survive of the six consecrated by the Patriarch. They claim two hundred and fifty-five churches and chapels, and, educationally, are strong in high, middle, and vernacular schools. There is much hope, though they still stand up for their old errors, that they will come nearer to the truth, because they have a great regard for the sacred Scriptures in the vernacular. One weak point is the almost adoration they have for the Syriac

1 *i.e.*, Nazarenes.

version of the Holy Scriptures—namely, the ancient *Peshitta* or *Peschito*. This is a translation from the Hebrew and the Greek, and yet they are said to be undertaking a translation from it rather than from the original. Meanwhile, however, the Metrans encourage their people to read our Malayalam version, advice which places them above the Romans, who are forbidden the Word of God in the vernacular, our version being called "poisonous." The Jacobites pride themselves—certainly the leaders do—on being Monophysites. They claim that Antioch is the head of the Christian world, and would fain make their people believe that the whole Christian Church is coming to their faith. They still use the dead Syriac in their church services, and are strong in prayers to the Virgin and the Saints.

The non-Romans continued.—The Reformed "Church of St. Thomas."—We are now come down to our own day, a hundred years after the visit of Dr. Claudius Buchanan, from whose efforts and researches the whole course of their history since 1806 has been flowing, with many rapids and some deep pools, on to the open sea of the Truth. Before the arrival of the Patriarch, the reforming Metran, Mar Matthew Athanasius, had, as we saw, consecrated as his suffragan and successor Mar Thomas Athanasius, and had established a Reformation Association to carry on the movement which he had fostered. At the present time there are three Metrans at the head of the Reformed Church—namely, Titus Mar Thoma, his suffragan,

Titus Mar Thoma II. (with some other Kattanars, prepared for the ministry in the Cambridge Nicholson Divinity Class under Rev. J. J. B. Palmer, now Archdeacon of Cottayam), and the Bishop of Anyura, in British Malabar. This Church calls itself the "St. Thomas Syrian Church," owns a hundred and seventeen churches and chapels, and at present probably numbers one-fourth of the whole, or sixty thousand, and has about two hundred Kattanars.

A Sunday in a Syrian Town: Good Work.—Both the Jacobite and the Reformed believe in Sunday schools and prayer meetings. Some years ago I happened to be in Mavelikara for Malayalam revision in connection with the New Testament, and I had "a Sunday off." This gave me the opportunity of seeing what our Syrian brethren were doing. First, I was taken by a matriculate teacher in the local State school to the Sunday School which he was conducting for sixty Syrian boys and girls, properly divided up into classes, and many of them having Malayalam Bibles. I was allowed to examine them, and was well satisfied with what I saw. Then, about eleven o'clock, I attended service in the Syrian Church, which was performed in the vernacular according to the Reformed Liturgy, accompanied by Malayalam hymns in native style such as we use in our mission churches. The service was concluded by a sermon. The body of the church was occupied by men, the women being at the west end. The same evening, before sunset, walking with my wife

KACHĒRI OR "CUTHERRY" LANDING PLACE, COTTAYAM, WITH STEPS UP TO THE MAGISTRATES' AND OTHER COURT HOUSES.

The roofs of the boats are in sections, and the middle and the ends can be removed at pleasure—according to the weather. If the weather be stormy the whole is covered, and the boatmen, generally two, sleep until it is fine—time is no object.

through the main street, we came across two crowded prayer meetings held in native houses, many of the audience being seated in the open air, while the priest sat in the verandah and expounded the Scriptures. I was kindly pressed into taking part and speaking a word of exhortation at one of these meetings.

The Syrian laity have taken a large part in the effort for spiritual life, backing up their clergy in reformation, and now and then reacting on the Anglican Church also.

> "*There was a man, though some did count him mad—*
> *The more he gave away the more he had!*"

One exceptionally interesting case of an earnest layman was the rich farmer, Pūthiōtta Jacob. Like many earnest Syrians, when occasion offered, he would attend the services in the Church Missionary Society's churches. He was present one Sunday morning in Cottayam church when the second lesson happened to be from the book of Revelation. After service he made his way into the vestry with twenty rupees (florins in size and value) and a "George and dragon" sovereign—a very rare coin in the "seventies"—and begged that the money might be devoted to local mission work, to fulfil, as he said, the promises of the sacred Book. I gladly received the offering, although some of his Syrian friends present entered a protest, declaring that he was mad. However, I undertook to await his further and more sober wishes; but instead of repenting of his liberality, he made more valuable offerings, amounting to about £40, for the preaching of the Gospel among the heathen. He took also great interest in the evangelizing of the "freedmen" working on his estate. On one occasion this good man presented a large supply of *Vino Sacro*, procured direct from England, for the purpose of Holy Communion among the Reformers.

Evangelizing of the Heathen by the Reformed Syrians.—The Reforming Syrians make constant efforts at evangelizing,[1] and are always to be found busy at the annual preachings at Ochira, in the south, and the all-night effort at Alwaye, near Cochin, when the Church Missionary Society's missionaries and catechists seek the salvation of the multitudinous Hindus assembled for their great festivals. Some spiritually minded Jacobite priests may sometimes be met with on the same field-days, carrying out "the Lord's marching orders." Roman Catholics never, to my knowledge, preach to the heathen in the open air.

The Reformers have borne a part in the revision of the Malayalam of the New Testament, completed in 1898, and since then have been taking their share in that of the Old Testament, just completed, and they are very hearty in supporting the Bible Society.

They have for several years held a convention annually near Mārāmannu, for the deepening of the spiritual life—a suitable object in a suitable place, close to the birth-place of the Syrian Reformation.

---

[1] They have already 1,577 converts from the heathen.

A Convention.—The following account was written by me some years ago, and describes one of these gatherings:—

"A remarkable scene, truly. The dry bed of a great river in Travancore, an area of tawny sand fully a furlong wide, and people in white, with books in their hands, thronging to one point. On the high banks, fifty feet above, are the lofty coconut palms and other shady trees with evergreen verdure. A church or two, with the remarkable chancel roofs higher than the nave, betokening 'Syrian Christians'' places of worship; comfortable farmhouses and clergy homes are dotted about, and not very far away may be detected the gilded pinnacle of a temple devoted to the worship of a Hindu god. But the crowds are hastening to no stone-built church, nor heathen temple. Their goal is a large booth erected on the dry sand of a river bed, and evidently intended for a great audience, for there are no fewer than one hundred and fifty pillars, *areca* palm-stems, and the meetings are to be prolonged into the night, since one hundred lamps hang from the roof of palm leaves.

"There is to be a 'convention,' and the many assembled (estimated at twenty-five thousand), mostly men, are Syrian Christians, met to hear the Word of God at the mouth of a C.M.S. Missionary, Mr. Walker, of Tinnevelly.

"Just as the Syrian Metran, in 1806, invited the Church of England to rescue his people from the woeful ignorance of the Word of God, so the present reforming Metropolitan, Titus Mar Thoma, has requested the Rev. Thomas Walker to come and teach his people the 'way of holiness'; and here they are, priests, deacons, and people in their thousands, in this large structure, sitting, as is their custom, on the floor, with their Bibles, and in rapt attention. But, so spacious is the 'tabernacle,' and so large the audience, that, as my friend Archdeacon Oomen Mamen tells me, the interpreter's words had to be repeated by another half way down the booth, so as to reach the extreme limits of the hearers. The convention, which lasted for several days, ended with a collection of a thousand rupees, in Travancore practically £100, for the purposes of the Syrian Church Evangelistic Association. Some women put into the collection large earrings of wrought gold, worth £3 or £4 each, and others golden rings. My friend exclaims:

'Was not this Pentecostal? Pray tell the C.M.S. that they conferred a great boon on the poor Syrian Church by sending dear Mr. Walker, who is alike beloved and esteemed by both parties' (*i.e.*, by the Reformers and non-Reformers in the Syrian Church) 'and by our own people.'"

This was not the first time that such gatherings have taken place, but none under such quite satisfactory conditions had come to my notice. The late Rev. E. Bacheler Russell conducted conventions in various parts, and the Rev. Gelson Gregson and Mr. Walker himself have also before now preached to the Syrians with God's manifest blessing. The Church Missionary Society's secretary in Ceylon, the Rev. A. E. Dibben, speaking at a clerical meeting at Cottayam in 1906, said: "I have had the great pleasure lately, in Palamcottah, of addressing a larger number of native Christians than I had ever met before—namely, fourteen hundred. Imagine my astonishment and pleasure when I addressed fourteen thousand the other day in the Syrian convention!"

Thus the Lord has borne witness in due time to the Word of His Grace, and we find the ancient "Church of St. Thomas," at the beginning of the twentieth century, revived, and in a very different state from that in which it was when the Syrian Bishop invited the help of the English Church a century ago. The educational policy of the Church Missionary Society has been most fruitful of results. There are now large numbers of Syrian graduates, and hundreds of undergraduates, who have been pupils in her Scriptural schools, and are now employed in various church and mission schools, and some are holding important civil offices in the Mysore and British services, as well as in the Native States of Travancore and Cochin. A few have worked for Christ in Madras, and in the north as far as Masulipatam, and one or two in the Central Provinces. Just now (1907) one of the Jacobite clergy is an M.A. of the Madras University, a degree which in India has a higher examination following on the B.A. The power of the Church Missionary Society to influence even the Jacobites has not passed away when even their deacons, if only a few, are willing to study in our Divinity School. The day is surely at hand when the Syrians of Malabar should be the missionaries of South India. Let us pray earnestly that God will still bless His Word amongst them, and answer the prayers and further the efforts carried on for now a hundred years.

A stirring among Roman-Syrians through a New Testament.—As an instance of life stirring among the Roman-Syrians, even in spite of their Jesuit rulers, I give one instance well known to me. A Roman-Syrian priest was vicar of a parish near Alleppey. I gave his younger brother a Malayalam New Testament. Some time afterwards I heard that, as the result of this gift, the priest was preaching the Gospel. I went and encouraged him, and found him full of the belief that the Pope was anti-Christ. Later, he was visited by his Roman Bishop, who held a "meditation" (dhyānam, perhaps "retreat"), at which a bonfire was made of such vernacular Scriptures as were given up by some of the flock. The priest and a hundred families remained firm, and made overtures to join our church under Bishop Hodges, but they were not received. Once, on a Sunday morning, I preached in his large church, surrounded in the pulpit by images which he had deposed from the church walls, etc. The priest went on persevering in his anti-Roman attitude, and tried to hold possession of the church against his Bishop, who carried the case to the law-courts, with the result that the vicar was defeated, and betook himself to the Nestorians[1] at Trichur. Some of his parishioners near Alleppey started as a new parish under his curate, and near the old site; they also claiming to be Nestorians. Others of his old Roman flock became Jacobites, and others joined the Reformed St. Thomas Christians; so there are four sections of the Syrians represented in that one spot—Roman-Syrians, Nestorians, Jacobites, and Reformed, all episcopal.

1 A small body of about 8,000, mostly at Trichur, in the Cochin State, who have left the Roman-Syrians.

CHAPTER VIII.

Chiefly about Bishops

Roman-Syrian Native Bishops.—Roman-Syrians have never settled down under the supremacy of foreign bishops. Their history, if we had time or space to tell it, would show a constant effort to obtain from the Portuguese and Roman authorities bishops of Syrian descent as their rulers, though under obedience to Rome. At length they carried their point, and in the year 1896 three Roman-Syrian priests were consecrated as bishops of titular sees, and sent to Travancore and Cochin as Vicars-Apostolic directly subject to the Pope of Rome for the management of their jurisdictions. All the Roman-Syrians are under these Metrans. In another matter they have preserved their ecclesiastical liberty, in that they are allowed the use of the Syriac language in their churches. Surely it is remarkable that the English and the other civilized nations, as well as the most unlettered tribes in India and the islands of the sea, are compelled, if Roman Catholics, to have their prayers in Latin, while these Syrians and some Greek communities are permitted to use the language of their ancestors. Alas! Syriac, Greek, and Latin

Mar Abd'Esa
Formerly a Roman Catholic.

Mar Dionysius,
Metropolitan.

Mar Julius Alvarez.
Formerly a Roman Catholic.

Group of Six Jacobite Metrans, and some Kattanars and Deacons.

Ever since the visit of the Jacobite Patriarch the priests wear black or dark cassocks.

are equally "unknown tongues" to the common people.

Secessions from Latins to Jacobite Syrians.—The Jacobites were increased in numbers and influence by the following circumstances. There had been, by Papal grant dating from the sixteenth century, an arrangement called the Padroado (patronage), which allowed to the Kings of Portugal the right of nominating bishops to dioceses of the Roman Church in India (some of which, if not all, would be in British territory). Anyhow this was inconvenient, and in 1886 was abolished by a Concordat between Pope Leo XIII. and the King of Portugal. The change became, however, the cause of much dissatisfaction to several Roman congregations of natives in South India, who suddenly found themselves, by a stroke of the pen, transferred to the jurisdiction of Italian prelates. A certain Father Alvarez, of the Roman Church under the Archbishop of Goa, and who had been a Brahman, was the head of some such dissidents. He applied to the Jacobite Bishops in Malabar for episcopal consecration, and at Cottayam the ceremony was duly performed by three Metrans in 1888. Father Alvarez took the title of Mar Julius Alvarez, and was accepted as Bishop by some discontented congregations of the Roman Church in Ceylon and South India.

* * * * * * * * *

CHAPTER IX.

A Discussion—South India and St. Thomas

Could St. Thomas have preached in South India?—We naturally ask what reasons there are for believing that these Christians are really connected with St. Thomas, and is it likely or possible that the Apostle found his way into South India, unknown as it was to the European nations of the West at least until the fifteenth century?

This is an interesting subject for inquiry, and I propose to answer it by showing that *South India is itself a Bible land*, and was known to the nations anciently inhabiting the coasts of the Mediterranean Sea long before the Portuguese and nations further west knew of its existence.

King Solomon, we are told (1 Kings ix. 26-28), had a navy of ships in Ezion-Geber (on the Gulf of Akabah, at the head of the Red Sea), whence they traded under the pilotage of King Hiram's Phœnician seamen, "who had knowledge of the sea, to Ophir," or, as the Greek version, "The Septuagint," has it, to *Σωφιρα*, Sōphira. We are told (1 Kings x. 11) that these ships brought from Ophir "great plenty of almug trees," according to Dr. Tristram and Sir J. D. Hooker probably the *Pterocarpus santalinus*, the Indian red sandal wood. They also brought precious stones, for the abundance of which India has always been celebrated, the mines of Golconda being especially famous. In verse 22 we are further informed that "once in three years came the navy of Tarshish, bringing gold and silver, ivory, and apes, and peacocks." Here philology comes to our aid, and we learn that ivory is called in the Hebrew *shen-habbim*, *i.e.*, the teeth of elephants, *hab* being the Hebrew equivalent for *habh*, Sanskrit for *elephant*. But "apes and peacocks" are mentioned in the Hebrew Bible in their Indian names; *ape*, Hebrew *kop*, Sanskrit and Malayalam *kapi; peacock*, Hebrew *tukki*, Tamil name *tokei*. (See also 2 Chron. ix.) Gold has always been procured in India, and is at the present time being obtained from the Ghauts east of Malabar, where the English and Australian miners have come across extensive workings of ancient exhausted mines.

We see from these facts, pointed out years ago by several important authorities—the *Speaker's Commentary*, the Rev. Professor Sayce, etc., etc.—that the Hebrews and the Phœnicians in King Solomon's time, one thousand years before Christ, traded to a place called Ophir, whence Indian products were obtained and imported, *with Indian names*, into Palestine by the way of the Red Sea.

Now where was this Ophir? Why should it not also be known by an Indian name in the Bible? The *Speaker's Commentary* supposes that the foregoing facts would necessitate at least a port in Southern Arabia, which was an emporium of

Indian commerce. But why need there be any great "knowledge of the sea" merely to coast along the Arabian Peninsula towards the south to such a port?

Josephus tells us that King Solomon procured these things from the Aurea Chersonesus, *i.e.*, the gold peninsula, *c.f.*, our Gold Coast. This is defined by scholars to be India within the Ganges. He might easily have said Arabia, if he meant it. Now the Septuagint version of the Old Testament was made at Alexandria before the time of Josephus, and in the passages quoted above we find that the translators render *Ophir* as *Sōpheir*, *Souphir*, *Sōphira*, etc., and we find that there is a very ancient site on the western coast of India, thirty-five miles north of Bombay, and five miles north of Bassein, called by the name of *Sōpāra*, having at the present time two thousand people and six hundred houses.

This has been identified by Professor Benfey and other scholars with Ophir. The Aryo-Indian name Sōpāra was probably changed into Ophir by the Phœnicians or Hebrews, and in the Septuagint the Aryo-Greek language restores the *s*, and we find the form *S*ouphir, *S*ōphir, etc.

Sōpāra was formerly the capital of the kingdom of Aparānta, stretching from Navsari, north of Bombay, to Gōkarnam, the sacred northern city of Malabar (about lat. 15°). Sōpāra was anciently a great port, but the sea has receded some distance, as it has done all along the western coast of India;

but it is noted also as a holy city among the Brahmans, Buddhists, and Jains (as well as being the wealthy capital and emporium of Aparānta, or the Konkan), from 250 B.C. to A.D. 1500.

In the many writers who mention the name—and there are more than twenty—it always appears in a form almost identical with that found at the present day, and used in the LXX., that is, Sōpāra or Suppāra (LXX., Sopheir, etc.). Amongst others, Ptolemy, A.D. 137, and the author of the *Periplus of the Erythræan Sea*, A.D. 247, and the Greek monk, Kosmas Indikopleustes, speak of Sōpāra, assigning it to the locality of the town bearing that name at the present day.

Excavations made within the last two years prove the antiquity of the site, and a coin of an Indian king, A.D. 160, and quite new, which was found with some Buddha relics in an ancient mound, seem to conclude the matter as to the great age of Sōpāra.[1]

What is the sum of all this? Surely it appears that Ophir was an emporium for Indian merchandise, that the Greek form of the name was identical with "Sōpāra," the name of the ancient capital and emporium for the western coast of India, in whose mountains are found all the undoubted Indian products introduced by the navy of ships of Tarshish.

Hence we infer the identity of Ophir and Sōpāra.

---

1 See *Sōpāra and Padana*, Education Society's Press, Bombay.

(Some scholars think that Ophir was the name of a *region* in Southern and Western India.) India was thus well known to Palestine in the time of King Solomon. The Greeks from at least the second century of our era knew of the trade winds or monsoons.

Our Blessed Lord was laid in the new tomb of Joseph enwrapped in a σινδων, or Indian muslin. [See later editions of Liddell and Scott's *Great Lexicon.*]

There are further proofs of early *European* intercourse with India. In 1837 an iron box containing some hundreds of large gold coins, as fresh as if from the mint, were found in the bed of the Beypore river in Malabar. Col. W. H. Horsley, R.E., possessed several of these with the "image and superscription" of more than one Cæsar. I had once the pleasure of handling them; the earliest bears date 2 B.C., the latest is about A.D. 50. Buried not later than A.D. 70 in the floor or vicinity of some rich merchant's house, the strong monsoon torrent washed away the bank of the river in which they were buried, and at length they were found to enrich the treasuries or cabinets of the Indian princes on whose borders they were discovered. Again, five hundred and twenty-three Roman coins of a similar age were discovered in 1842 in the Coimbatore district east of the Ghauts.

These coins, too, probably formed part of the wealth of some foreign merchant. Arabs at the present day, in crazy dhows, cross the Arabian Sea, and bring dates, limes, hulwa, and other commodities, importing in exchange cardamoms and the many spices for which Malabar, known anciently as "the *pepper* coast," has been famous.

In the native town of Cochin, 10° north latitude, are two communities of "White" and "Black" JEWS. Jewish accounts on the spot tell us that 10,000 of the ancient people of God arrived on the coast A.D. 70, or soon after the destruction of the temple of Herod. Some suppose that the Black Jews are the descendants of a still earlier settlement; but it seems more likely, from the fact that these two communities do not intermarry, that the latter were originally the *slaves* of their White brethren. Jews will intermarry with proselytes; never, I am informed, with slaves. Both communities, highly respected, though much impoverished and diminished by the Portuguese persecution of the sixteenth century and by internal discords, maintain the synagogue worship and traditions of their fathers. (See also Buchanan's *Christian Researches.*)

Now it is easy to see that the Apostle St. Thomas *could* find his way to the Malabar coast, and it is very difficult to imagine that the Apostles of Christ should refrain from seeking to evangelize a country known to their ancestors, opened up to trade by the conquests of Alexander and by the voyages of Arabs, and destined to become, if not so at that day, a refuge for Jews.

The constant tradition of the Church, that St. Thomas was the Apostle of India, finds therefore abundant collateral evidence; and may we not see in such a fact the fulfilment of the Psalmist's prophecy: "At Thy right hand did stand the queen in gold of Ophir" (Ps. xlv. 9)?

CHAPTER X.

THE INDIAN STORY OF ST. THOMAS

Indian Christian tradition may now be heard. There is a very interesting account in *Malayalam*, the language of Malabar, which is non-Roman, and has been extant[1] since the middle of the eighteenth century, and, beginning with St. Thomas, brings the history of the Syrian Christians of Malabar down to A.D. 1770.

The story, which I have literally translated, is as follows:—

"In the Name of the Unoriginated and Endless Essence. When Chōra Perumāl ruled in Choramandal (east coast of India), one day in sleep, by the Divine blessing, the king beheld beautiful buildings like a palace, filled with light and splendour, and sights productive of beautiful thoughts. Filled with unbounded joy he awoke, and while very eagerly thinking over the matter, and making inquiries, he came across a certain merchant named Hāwān, and to him he related all these things, saying, 'I have a boundless desire to build myself just such a palace, and for this purpose you must procure me a skilful artificer.'

1 That is the MS. from which my transcript was taken.

The merchant accepted the royal charge, and promised, by the blessing of God, to find one. The king gave the money needed for the undertaking, and sent him on his journey, with attendants. He set out on the search, and at length came to Mahosa, in the land of Yūs.[1] While dwelling here in grief, the Lord Jesus Messiah appeared to him as a man of that country, and graciously promised all that he was so earnestly seeking, and said, 'I will give and send with you a master carpenter most highly skilled in all kinds of work.' Having heard the Divine word he was astonished, and forthwith, by the Spirit, Jesus summoned the Apostle Mar Thōmma, and said, 'Lo, there is the carpenter! He will accomplish everything according to your mind.' Then He sold the apostle to Hāwān for a sum of money, which He received and handed to the apostle. But when He ordered him to go with the merchant, the apostle declared his sorrow, and said, 'Two and two Thou didst send the others into all lands, but Thou hast commanded me into a land of malefactors whose tongues I know not, and who live like beasts of prey.' Jesus said, 'Fear not, I am with thee; thy thoughts are my thoughts.' - "Thus commanded and encouraged, Mar Thōmma the apostle departed with Hāwān, and in the year of our Lord 52 he arrived in Mylapūr [now part of Madras]. At the first interview with the king his majesty commanded him, saying, 'Draw

1 Yudia or Judæa?

a plan of the palace which I saw in my dream, in its extent and beauty, that I may know it.' Then the apostle drew the palace, and the king, seeing it, rejoiced and greatly honoured the apostle, and told him all about the work. The apostle assenting, all the details as to the site, the expense, and the necessary time were agreed upon, and the king gave him the required money, and commanded him to gather all things necessary and to build. He departed, and began to make known the Gospel, to gather the poor, to comfort them as they needed, to heal the sick, the demoniacs, the blind, and the lame. In those days, when the way of baptism was increasing, the devil entered into the hearts of his servants, and, being jealous, they informed the king that not a single stone was cut for the palace, nor even the foundation laid, and that all the vast wealth entrusted to the apostle was being squandered on those who joined his new religion; and that there was not the slightest sign of the building. When the king heard this he called the apostle and asked him, saying, 'How much of the palace is finished? Let me see all that you have done.' To which the apostle answered, 'The palace is quite finished, and it is in the heavenly kingdom, but the time has not come for you to behold it.'

"When the king heard this he was angry, and sent for Hāwān, and cast them both into prison. Then he bethought him how he might further ill-treat them, 'for by this affair,' reasoned he, 'I have incurred dishonour, an ill name, and loss of wealth.' So he was grieved, and his mind was disturbed, and a sickness broke out. The heir apparent died in the meanwhile, and by the Divine will angels received his spirit and carried him to bliss, where he saw a palace called 'The palace of the King built by Mar Thōmma.' The angels told him that the apostle had made this palace for the king, his brother, against the time when they should carry him to Paradise. Hearing this he rejoiced in spirit, and immediately, by the Lord's command, his soul was restored to his body, and he returned to life. Having called the king, his brother, he said, 'I am your brother. Deny me not what I shall ask of you.' The elder king replied, 'With great joy will I grant all that you ask.' When he had ceased speaking, he replied, 'My request is that you agree to receive of me all the money you have given for the building of the palace, with one in ten added, and that you give me in exchange the palace which the Hebrew has finished for you.' Thereupon the king, who had despaired [of the palace], asked with great desire to know his secret, and he told him the whole matter. Then the king rejoiced, but being greatly melted for his sinful conduct, they both went with reverence, saw the apostle, fell at his feet, did reverence, and loosed his bonds. With deep humility both the kings, and with them many people, received baptism. Then the apostle, after he had ordained many priests and built churches there, set out for several other countries and preached the Gospel.

"In the hill country of Chērakōn, in Malabar, in Kerala, in those days there was no king, but thirty-two *gramas* [village colonies of Brahmans] and thirty-two chiefs held sway.

"Accordingly, when the apostle disputed with them, the Truth won the victory,[1] and many from

"OLD CHURCH" STEPS.

various *gramas*, being convinced, believed and were baptized. In each of the two gramas, Shankarapuri and Pakalōnmattam,[2] he appointed

---

1 These appear to have been independent priest communities, and the people were free to act—more so than they could have been if they had a despotic monarch. There were thirty-two gramas in Chērakōn, but sixty-four in all Kerala.

2 The representatives and descendants of this family have borne office as Bishops up to the nineteenth century.

one priest; and, setting forth again, he preached the Way and made many people sons of baptism, and, by the name of the Infinite, he set up the Cross in Malabar and built these seven churches—Kōtta-kāyalil, Gōkamangalam, Niranam, Chayil, Kurakēni, Quilon, and Palūr. After this he itinerated in Malabar for thirty years, and having gone again to the Pāndi ['Choramandal'] country to preach the Gospel, on the way as he went an Embran [or Brahman], casting a dart, hit him, and he was buried in the Little Mount at Mylapur. Angels[1] carried him to Urāha (or Edessa). May his prayers be with us. Amen."

Such and so far is the native account of the introduction of Christianity by the Apostle St. Thomas into Malabar.

---

1 The word, which in the translated story is Syriac, may mean merely *Messengers*. In the hymns of St. Ephrem nothing is said which could mean that the transference of the Apostle's bones to Edessa was miraculous.

CHAPTER XI.

EARLY WRITERS AND KING ALFRED

If such an account as that just given stood alone, with no support from external history or tradition, we might be justified in rejecting it as unworthy of credit, but all along the ages St. Thomas has been known as the Apostle of India, as is shown by the following, quoted or adapted from the interesting pamphlet[1] by the late learned Rev. C. Egbert Kennet, D.D.:—

"In A.D. 190 the celebrated Pantœnus, who presided over the Alexandrian School and travelled from Syria to India, is reported (by Eusebius, Bishop of Jerusalem) 'to have found his own arrival anticipated by some who were acquainted with the Gospel of Matthew, to whom Bartholomew, one of the Apostles, had preached, and had left them the same Gospel in the Hebrew, which was also preserved unto this time.'"

This extract shows that in some parts of *India* Christianity had been preached by an Apostle. The Syrian Christians hold that the persons who told Pantœnus said "Mar Toma" (Lord or Bishop Thomas), which was misunderstood as Bar Tolmai. The same incident is related by St. Jerome (A.D. 390), but he also mentions of our Saviour that "He was present in all places—with Thomas in

---

[1] *St. Thomas, the Apostle of India*, Second Edition, Madras, 1892.

India, with Peter in Rome, with Paul in Illyria," etc., etc., showing that, whatever might have been held about St. Bartholomew, St. Jerome fully believed that St. Thomas was the Apostle of India. Bishop Dorotheus (born A.D. 254) says that the Apostle Thomas suffered martyrdom at Calamina, a town in India. This is supposed to be *Kallumēl ninnu*, "from the top of the rock," referring to St. Thomas' Mount, near Madras; but the name has had other explanations.

Gregory Nazianzen (A.D. 370) witnesses that as Paul had to do with the Gentiles, so "John with Ephesus, Thomas with India."

St. Gregory of Tours (A.D. 544-595) tells how at a "place in India, where the body of Thomas lay before it was transported to Edessa, there is a monastery," and a miracle is recorded, etc. Thus we see how well-known it was, about the time when St. Augustine was preaching to our Anglo-Saxon ancestors in Canterbury, that the Apostle Thomas had been buried in India, and that his body was afterwards carried to Edessa, which agrees with the Malayalam story.

In A.D. 547 Kosmas, an Alexandrian monk from the very city of Pantœnus, and who was called *Indikopleustes* because of his voyages to India, says:—

"In Ceylon (Taprobana) an island of further India, where the Indian Ocean reaches, there is found a Christian church with clergy and laity, whether further I do not know. Similarly in Male, as they call it, whence Malabar, where pepper is produced. In Calliana, however (so they tell me), there is a bishop usually ordained in Persia."

The Malabar coast is the land of pepper, and Calliana may be the town of Quilon, where we know that *two* Persian bishops arrived in 825. Dr. Kennett thinks, however, that Calliana is the territory of that name between Bombay and Goa.

Our own Alfred the Great, in 883, as recorded in the *Anglo-Saxon Chronicle*, sent an embassy to India, headed by Sighelm, Bishop of Shireburn, "bearing the alms which the King had vowed to send . . . to India to St. Thomas and to St. Bartholomew." The embassy "penetrated with great success to India, and brought thence many foreign gems and aromatic liquors."

The deeply interesting tradition of St. Thomas as the Apostle of India, although it may have been made use of for purposes of superstition by the Portuguese, is altogether non-Roman, and dates from the purest ages of the Church, and has been continuously held from the earliest times, as we have it on evidence dating from the second century. It is ratified by the existence of an episcopal church, as well as by the facts of the Jewish colonies on the Malabar coast, and the intercourse shown to exist between this very part of India and the land of Palestine three thousand years ago. The Jewish and Syrian inscriptions on copper documents, and the Christian inscriptions on stone in a language unwritten in India for over a thousand years, also emphasize the tradition.

Now looking at the native story as it is thus simply given in the Malayalam, it is much more dignified than the prolix and improbable *acts of*

St. Thomas in the apocryphal "Acts of the Apostles." One or two points deserve special notice. There seems to be no more of miracle in the story than might be expected during the era of supernaturally endowed apostles. The dream of the heathen king, the appearance and words of the Lord, taken with the corresponding object of this appearance—namely, the evangelisation of a heathen people—are they very unworthy when put side by side with the miracles recorded in the inspired Acts of the Apostles? Then this is in favour of the truthfulness of the account, so unlike what one might expect, that the work of the apostle, like the speech of the proto-martyr, is unfinished. He left but two ordained men behind him, not a fully organised church, with bishops, priests, and deacons. The after relapse of some of the people into sorcery and heathenism is all in keeping with the above, and has the appearance of simple truth. Again, though in great straits for want of clergy, we do not find these primitive Christians of Malabar setting up a Church government, or ordaining, *sine episcopo*—they abide God's time.

CHAPTER XII.

Indian Story Continued

The Malabar tradition continues thus:—

"Now as long as the two persons ordained by the Apostle St. Thomas lived, all the Christians that were in Kurakēni, Quilon, etc., and as far as Palūr walked agreeably to the practices of the faith; but when those clergy passed away they were distressed. At that time the highly necessary sacraments of marriage and baptism began to be performed in a less regular way by the head-men [lay elders].

"So after a long time had elapsed, and because the country was full of paganism, and there was no one to teach the revealed religion, and by reason of familiarity with pagan stories and fables, some learnt songs, odes, and incantations inconsistent with the Faith, and attended the temple feasts and listened to the worship and made secret offerings to the gods. At that time Mānikka Wāchakar,[1] a sorcerer, led astray, and with the royal force and authority persecuted, the Christians that were in Chōramandal. This sorcerer came

[1] Incorrectly supposed to be a disciple of Manes. The late Rev. Dr. G. U. Pope has shown that Mānikka Wāchakar was a Hindu, and a restorer of Siva-ism in Southern India.

into Malabar, and by his witchcraft against the Christians, many families, in Kurakēni from Kottar to Quilon, he brought diseases upon them and pestilence on their cattle; and he said that if they summoned him, and caused sacred ashes to be put on, these afflictions would cease, and if they learnt the five letter incantation of the sages and other like things, and drank the milk, buttermilk, ghee,[1] cowdung, etc., the five sacred products of the cow, mixed together, they would have children. Now there were many people in the sixty-four [gramas] who would do none of these things, nor put on heathen ashes; but ninety-six households, which had multiplied from the members of eight families, did learn the five letter and other incantations, forsook God and joined with Mānikka Wāchakar, and these people are called the Manigrama unto this day; but those who for God's sake suffered all the evils brought upon them by this sorcery, and who would neither listen to the incantations nor put on the heathen ashes, a much larger number among the sixty-four (gramas), these Mānikka Wāchakar and the people who followed him called Dhariāykkal (non-wearers), and therefore they are still so called. Now two hundred and ninety-three years from the arrival of Mar Thomas the Apostle, at which time these people were becoming more and more afflicted, by the blessing of God, Who saw the decay of the Christians, the Bishop of Urāha,[2] in the land of

---

[1] Clarified butter. [2] Urāha is Edessa in Asia Minor.

Syria, had this dream-oracle in his sleep, as follows: 'Is it no sorrow to you that the Christians of Malabar, whom I died to gain, are wasting and perishing?' Having heard this voice, the Bishop of Urāha went to the holy Katholikos[1] of Jerusalem, and reported the matter. Then the Katholikos called together all the experienced divines, and having taken counsel with them and come to a decision, he summoned an honourable Christian merchant named Thōmma, living in Jerusalem, and commanded him to ascertain and report the state of affairs in Malabar. He arrived in Malabar, and when he saw the cross worn as the badge of the Christians that believed through the labours of St. Thomas he approached them.

"He then inquired and learnt all their affairs in past years, and having seen their distress for want of clergy, he decided to make no stay there, but forthwith embarked in his ship, returned to Jerusalem, and told the holy Katholikos all their circumstances.

"Thereupon the Katholikos commanded and sent with the honoured merchants, Joseph the Bishop of Urāha, and besides him several priests and deacons, and many men, women, and children. Having blessed them, he embarked them, and, by the mercy of God, they all landed safe at Malabar in the year of our Lord 345.

"Then the people in the division of Kottakāyal, and the Christians, called Dhariāykkal (non-wearers), in the sixty-four (gramas), assembled, and

1 Ecclesiastical Patriarch.

having taken counsel together they submitted to the Bishop. Afterwards Knayil Thōmma paid a visit to the royal presence of Chērumān Perumāl, the sovereign king of Malabar, and presented an offering, and declared all the circumstances. Then his majesty was glad, and made declaration as follows: 'All that is required of us, the ruler of the land, we have no hesitation in granting, and according thereto the sun and the moon are witnesses, so that as long as sun and moon endure there shall never be any breach in this grant of the following necessary privileges: to wit [here follows a list of seventy-two outward marks of distinction enjoyed by the Brahmans and high castes in Malabar, some relate to houses, some to processions, some to ornaments and dress], and other rights consequent thereupon and included in the above. . .' These he caused to be engraved on copper.

"Then the land of Kodungallur, within Parawalannyi, measuring two hundred and forty-four rods of elephant measure, and by the authority of Chērakōn Tēwarira, ruling as prince, with flowers and water (signs of possession), were received by the foreign Christian, Thōmma, and recorded. In this manner he planted a stake for a church and a town on the following auspicious date, A.D. 345, in the 11th month (Aquarius), the 29th day, Saturday, and the 9th asterism and the 7th day.

"At that time, in the sign of Cancer, having received Kodungallur, the town called Mahadevar-pattanam (the city of the Great God), and while he was dwelling there with festoons and might, he cleared out the enemies that were struggling for the sovereignty in Malabar, and for this object laid out necessary wealth, making great exertions, and having crowned Chēramān Perumāl as lord to reign, and having presented him with the upheaped measure of jewels for his crown, it was therefore commanded that no one till the end of the world should do any dishonour to this people.

"For this and other purposes he gave and sent with us seventeen castes, which are necessary to other castes. These seventeen castes were in India (Bāratha) before the time of (the low-caste sage) Pakanār. These seventeen he gave to those who were baptized to do low work (or to be inferior)." [Then follow the names of the low castes—blacksmiths, carpenters, etc., etc.] "These (Christians) abounding in faultless goodness, for protection united with their greatness the Manigrāma. If the people of any caste did any injury, whether barons or princes, with temple power or civil power, against one of these eighteen castes, if the eighteen castes assembled and deliberated, they would not be appeased until a fine was paid. This was the practice for nine hundred and twenty years, but now (1770) they do not so take counsel together. In this way the Nasrānis (Nazarenes), who came from Jerusalem with their honours and good customs, having taught us (the Gospel), became joined with us in marriage, but similarly, lest degeneracy of race should take place, the great ones united together the enslaved among those who came (from Syria) and the inferior people (of this country), and built one hundred houses of one kind in the northern row, and the inferior ones seventy-two of another kind on the south side, and that there may be no change herein for all generations, the greater hold the succession on the father's side, and the inferior on the mother's." Here follow the differing customs. "The great ones marry standing, the inferior kneeling; the great ones' ornament is the cross, the inferior ones' the *chalawam* in marriage. The great ones veil (the bride) all over, the inferior ones only the shoulders. The great ones at a marriage give sweetmeats immediately after the wedding, the inferior ones before, etc., etc. The merchandise of the great ones is gold and silver, that of the inferiors salt, fish, etc. Thus for great ones and inferiors were customs of distinction settled, and the city was named Maha Dēwar Pattanam, and called after Jerusalem, the city of God.

"Now, before the Nasrānis, children of God, settled down there, Knāyi Thomman[1] and the Bishop and malpans (divines) having taken counsel together, thought it not right to take away the ruling power from the family to whom Mar Thomas the Apostle gave ordination to rule all the Christians in Malabar, therefore they gave the dignity of Archdeacon to that family to rule all

---

[1] The same as Thomma, before-mentioned, and called also Thomas of Cana.

the people and to have pre-eminence. Accordingly, in all periods they exercised judicial powers on all the Malabar Christians while bishops were constantly coming from Antioch, and they all gave authority in Malabar to the archdeacons (arkadayākōns). They ruled all Malabar (diocese) for four hundred and eighty years. Afterwards the Portuguese (Paranki or Feringhee) came to Cochin Fort, and thereby the coming of the Bāwās[1] [the Patriarchs from Babylon] was put a stop to."

In this account there is given an explanation of the fact that among the Syrians there were two parties, the "Northerns" and the "Southerns," of whom the Northerns were supposed to be the highest. They never intermarried until in 1872 a young man of the "Southerns," a student in our college, married a Northern girl. He became eventually a pastor in our Church, of which, at the time of his marriage, his father-in-law was a very active member, and he died the death of a good shepherd—for his flock.

[1] *Bawa*, Syriac for father = papa or Pope, and hence patriarch, the highest ecclesiastical title.

CHAPTER XIII.

AN OBJECTION DISCUSSED

The Rev. George Milne Rae, in his book, *The Syrian Church in India*,[1] aiming to show that the Apostle St. Thomas preached only in India north of the Ganges, and not in the south, goes on to say, with reference to the Malayalam-Syrian tradition of Brahmin converts made by the Apostle in Travancore, "It is sufficient to remark that in the second century (A.D.) there were neither Jews, Christians, nor Brahmins in Malabar."

Let us consider the question of the Brahmins, the chief Aryan-speaking people in India, who must have introduced their language into Southern India, where, especially in the Malayalam country, it has greatly enriched the language. The learned Bishop Caldwell says: "The oldest Dravidian word found in any written records of the world appears to be the word 'peacock' in the Hebrew text of the books of Kings and Chronicles, in the list of the articles of merchandise brought in Solomon's ships about 1000 B.C." "Dravidian" means one of the South Indian or non-Aryan languages. The word *tokei*, to which Bishop

---

1 Black & Sons, Edinburgh.

Caldwell refers, would only be used in South India. If *peacocks* were imported into Palestine from North India they would bear a Sanskrit name, or if from Ceylon a Pali name, and peacocks are plentiful all over India and Ceylon, and have Aryan names.

This seems to place the port of embarkation in the Tamil country, where St. Thomas first, according to the legend, began his work, and where he was eventually martyred.

"Elephant" in Hebrew is *hab*, the equivalent of the Sanskrit *habh;* and "ape" is *kap*, for the Sanskrit *kapi*, a name still used in Travancore for "monkey": *Kaviur*, or *Kapiur*, "monkey land," being the name of a well-known place in Travancore from whose hills the *apes* were exported. These are Aryan words.

These words, then, go to prove that Aryans were living in South India 1000 B.C., side by side with Dravidians. If so, why not in A.D. 53, or somewhat later, when St. Thomas is reported to have converted them?

In Psalm xlv. 8, the Divine Bridegroom is described as clad in robes smelling of "myrrh, aloes, and cassia." Professor Earle quoted in *Dean Kirkpatrick* on the *Psalms* notes that "these English spice names are all identical with the words in the Hebrew: 'For with these Oriental spices their Oriental names travelled westward, and they became, through Greek and Latin, the common property of the European languages.'" *Myrrh* is Arabic; *cassia* is the *koost* of India

(Indian orris); *aloes* is the perfumed wood of an Indian tree. Ivory is also mentioned in the same connection with "gold of Ophir." This note is given here because it well illustrates the way in which words carry historical evidence.

The strongest point against South India as the scene of the Apostle's labours is that the *Acts of St. Thomas* relates that he was summoned to India by Gondaphares, an Indo-Parthian king, and not by a South Indian raja. But, on the other hand, what weight need we attach to the report of a writer who attributes all sorts of unscriptural and Gnostic practices to the Apostle? The "*Acta*" has been altered by later writers to make the facts fit in with the views of a Gnostic age.

It is not impossible that St. Thomas, or some other apostle, may have made converts and established churches in other parts of India. We know that the Christians of St. Thomas have left Calicut, where they first met the Portuguese, and were driven out of Cranganore (Kodungallur or Mahadevar-pattanam). May it not be that earlier settlements to the north were forsaken or destroyed under the stress of persecution? One of the seven churches founded by St. Thomas was at a place named Chayal, in the eastern hills of Travancore. It has long been abandoned owing to wild animals; but the ruins remain, and would repay antiquarian research.

Fresh light of a most interesting kind has been thrown upon the question in a laborious and considerable volume by the Right Rev. Bishop

A. E. Medlycott, formerly Vicar-Apostolic of the Roman See at Trichur, in the Cochin state, north of Travancore. In his book[1] (I quote from an article by myself in the *Church Missionary Review* for 1907, p. 651)—

"Bishop Medlycott says, with a certain amount of truth, that it is the *odium theologicum* which has made many writers so ready to doubt the Church traditions assigning Southern India as the mission-field of the Apostle Thomas, and to contradict also the beliefs of the Syrian Christians of Malabar that they themselves are the descendants of his first converts there. The latest considerable writer before Bishop Medlycott is the Rev. G. Milne Rae, in his book, *The Syrian Church.* He claims to have shown that the St. Thomas Christians are merely Syrian colonists who arrived in India in the end of the sixth century, and he believes that he has proved this by a discussion of certain coins bearing the name of Gondophares, who reigned in Cabul from about A.D. 20 to 60. St. Thomas the Apostle is connected with this king by Bardesanes, the writer of an ancient Syriac work known as *Acta Thomæ.* Therefore, argues Rae, St. Thomas's India must have been N.-W. India or Afghanistan exclusively.

"Bishop Medlycott, while accepting the missionary labours of the Apostle St. Thomas in the neighbourhood of King Gondophares, holds that he afterwards preached and was martyred in Southern India at St. Thomas' Mount, near Madras. The evidence on which he bases his belief is very interesting.

"St. Ephrem Syrus (who died A.D. 370), in his Syriac hymns written at Edessa and Nisibis in Asia Minor, refers to the labours of the Apostle St. Thomas among 'the Indians,' upon whose 'sun-burnt' and 'dark' complexions the saintly poet dwells. The bones of St. Thomas, brought from India to Edessa, he sings of as 'valuable treasure'—'this *pearl*, none greater doth India yield.'

"The argument is this—If St. Ephrem thought that Afghanistan (or King Gondophares' regions), *in the same*

1 *India and the Apostle Thomas*, by A. E. Medlycott, Bishop of Tricomia. London: David Nutt, 1905.

latitudes as Edessa, was the place whence the relics of the Apostle had come, how could he describe their people as *dark* or *sun-burned*, and what would be the fitness of alluding to a *pearl?* This, on the other hand, would well suit with South India, near Ceylon, where the inhabitants are dark-complexioned, and where the famous pearl-fisheries are worked to this day. These and similar considerations do not, perhaps, absolutely prove that the India of St. Thomas was in the southern Presidency, though it goes very near it. St. Ephrem, as the Bishop says, stands in these hymns for all his fellow-Christians of nearly sixteen centuries ago, and testifies to the common belief in Asia Minor in those days. Many similar references are quoted from early liturgical books, calendars, and martyrologies of the Eastern and Western Churches, but they are of less importance as being only *echoes* of the earliest belief.

"Then the chief visitors or reports of visitors to the reputed shrine of St. Thomas near Madras are given, Theodorus, A.D. 590, being the first, who is reported by St. Gregory of Tours. Then come the embassy of our Alfred the Great, 883; Ser Marco Polo, 1293; and various Roman ecclesiastics, 1324, 1349, 1430; and, finally, Nestorian bishops, 1504, about the date of the first arrival of the Portuguese in India, when, to say the least, the last began to darken the ancient local traditions herein by words without knowledge.

"To speak of the first of these names. The Indian and the Edessene date for the Feast of the Apostle St. Thomas, July 3rd, is made to yield a very clear proof that St. Gregory's informant, Theodore, had visited Mylapore and St. Thomas' Mount, Madras, for it was at the time of exceptionally heavy rains, such as never occur in Edessa, to which, as we saw above, the remains of the Apostle were carried, and where, as well as at Mylapore, a shrine or tomb of St. Thomas had been erected. The heavy rain was that of the south-west monsoon, and indicates that Theodore had visited the South Indian shrine of the Apostle, and that so far back as A.D. 590.

"The claims of others to be the Apostles of India are discussed and rejected, and a very exhaustive examination of the *Acts of St. Thomas* is given. From this we are led to see that the original story of the Apostle's career has been corrupted by

Gnostic interpolations, making him practically a Gnostic, and describing him as constantly forbidding the marriage of Christian lay people. There are, however, clear indications that the story is laid in a Hindu country, and *that* in the south; a land of ceremonial bathing before food, of prostration by noble ladies in the presence of heathen priests (? Brahmans), of vehicles drawn by cattle (not by horses), and of palanquins used to carry persons of distinction. Altogether the evidence seems to point strongly to a South Indian Apostolate of St. Thomas."

✠

T. Stokes, D.D., Professor of Ecclesiastical History in the University of Dublin, writing about St. Patrick, says: "I do not think any sound historical instinct will doubt that the tradition of a whole nation, embodied in documents some as old as the seventh century, and reproducing itself in the most permanent of all records—the topography of the country, must have had a solid foundation in fact: and that tradition ascribes our national conversion to one definite person—St. Patrick. The internal evidence is all in favour of its authenticity." Dr. Todd, speaking of the "Confessions" of St. Patrick, says: "It contains none of the ridiculous miracles which the later biographers of St. Patrick love to record."[1]
"*Change but a name, the tale is thine.*"

Let any Syrian of Malabar read "St. Thomas the Apostle" for "St. Patrick," and the coincidence amounts almost to identity.

---

[1] *Ireland and the Celtic Church*, Lecture ii., p. 25. S.P.C.K., 1907.

CHAPTER XIV.

SPECIMENS

An Account of a Syrian Reformed Service and of a Book of Prayers.—Cottayam is the head-quarters alike of the Syrians and of the Church Missionary Society, and being there (in 1905) on Sunday, August 21st, after Holy Communion at our early service, I attended the *Kurubāna* or Eucharist in one of the two Syrian reformed churches in the town. The vicar is a priest who, for the sake of primitive and Scriptural truth, has lost at law the largest church[1] in the place, which, with its endowments, has gone to the Jacobites. The new church built by the reformed congregation has, like many Syrian churches, three arches at the east end, each with its veil. The priest and communicants were, according to their custom, *fasting*. One cross stood above, another on, the "altar." The priest was assisted on the north by a deacon in a white cassock, and on the south by the sexton, who was in lay dress and swinging a *censer*. The priest, *vested in a cope*, kept the *eastward* position, except when turning to the west he frequently blessed the people with the sign of the cross. Two *lighted* candles stood on the reredos, and they were blown out once, at the sermon. The incense bearer at

[1] The Cherya Palli, or "Little Church" (see page 3).

certain times kissed the corners or *horns* of the "altar," and in turn censed it, the priest, and the people. Sometimes the priest made *prostrations* before the "altar." Most interesting of all was the "Kiss of Peace," given thus: The priest held both hands in the smoke of the censer, and then turned them towards the deacon, who drew them gently through his own, and offered his in turn to the nearest man, and so the "Kiss" was passed rapidly through the whole church.

Before the Eucharist, the priest said, in the words of the Liturgy, "Let the pure draw nigh"; the sexton in turn called out, "Let the prepared come forward," and then six or seven aged women came up, and kneeling in a line on the south side in the nave were communicated in both kinds, the wine being poured into their mouths from a spoon.

Now I had never before witnessed a Reformed *Kurubāna* from beginning to end—we have too much occupation with our own flocks—and it was a revelation to me. Here are the famous "Six Points" in full use in a Reformed Syrian Church, and yet the Church Missionary Society has been charged with altering the Syrian ceremonies, with which, indeed, we had nothing to do, nor could we have interfered if we desired or had the time.

From what I have heard, I gather that there is no rigid uniformity among the Reformed Syrians in the matter of ritual, and it is alleged against them as a proof of weakness; but it must be understood that they have not as yet had sufficient

RIVER SCENERY: STONE AND GIRDER BRIDGE NEAR OLESHA, COTTAYAM.
Young elephant drinking. A dangerous spot in flood-time.

time, and rest from lawsuits to elaborate their rules in matters of secondary importance.

In what follows, I give the first few pages of a book put forward by the Reformed Metran in Malayalam. Some prayers only are given here as specimens, but they are all equally good.

"ORTHODOX SYRIAN CHRISTIAN PRAYERS.

"Translated From Syriac, By Command Of The Most Reverend
"Mar Thomas Athanasius, Metropolitan
"of Malabar,
"Sitting On The Throne Of The Holy Apostle Mar Thomas.

"*OF PRAYER.*

"Taken from Canon V., section 5, commanded by the Holy Apostles, and orthodox Patriarchs.

"*We are commanded to pray standing, with faces towards the East, for at the last Messiah is manifested in the East.*

"2. *All Christians, on rising from sleep early in the morning, should at once wash the face and pray.*

"3. *We are commanded to pray seven times, thus: At morn, because the Lord granted light; at nine, because He was delivered to judgment; at noon, because He was nailed to the cross; at three, because the earth quaked and the dead rose; at eve, for rest during the night; at nine, for protection from dreams and apparitions of unclean spirits; at midnight, for safety and deliverance from all perils. If all cannot pray seven times, they are bound to pray thrice, as sometimes did David and Daniel.*

"4. *When a man prays, let him put his hands on his breast, control all his thoughts, and with reverence, attention, and humility, standing towards the East, let him worship with bowed head, and make the Cross, from forehead to breast, left shoulder to right, saying as follows:*—To Father, Son, and Holy Ghost be praise. From the beginning and for ever. Amen.

"Holy, Holy, Holy, is the Lord God, the Mighty One, with Whose praises are filled Heaven and Earth. In the Heights be praise. Blessed is He that hath come and shall come in the Name of the Lord. In the Heights be praise.

"O God, Holy art Thou. Mighty One, Holy art Thou. Deathless One, Holy art Thou. Thou Who didst hang upon the Cross for us, grant Thy blessing upon us. *Thus having said thrice, and having bowed thrice, let him say this following:—*

"O our Lord, grant Thy blessing upon us. Our Lord, with favour grant Thy blessing upon us. O our Lord, grant Thy blessing upon us, receiving our prayer and our service, grant Thy blessing upon us. Praise be to Thee, O Creator, Praise be to Thee. O Messiah, King, showing mercy upon Thy sinful servants, to Thee be praise. Barequmar (the Lord bless us).

"*THE LORD'S PRAYER.*

"*A Prayer* (against all dangers, ghostly and bodily). *Here, two—'Our Father' and Doxology; then say:*—O our Lord, Jesus Messiah, shut not Thou in our faces the door of Thy blessings. We confess that we are sinners, bless Thou us. Thy love brought Thee down from Thy place to us, that by Thy Death our death might be done away. Grant Thou Thy blessing upon us.

"*Here, after two—'Lord's Prayer' and two doxologies, say Psalm* 91, *Psalm* 121.

"*A Prayer* (for Protection). . . .

"*Having said this following, bow thrice.* An Act of Praise. . .

"*Say the Lord's Prayer, etc.*

"*Nicene Creed.*"

Then (in Syriac) Barequmar (the Lord bless us). Staumen kalos (let us stand well). Kuriyelayison (Lord have mercy). The last two phrases are Greek, though said as Syriac.

A prayer. (Against all evil thoughts, lusts, idle words, etc., etc.)

This is the Evening Prayer, and so the Syrian Church begins the day as the Jews did, in the evening. Prayers for other hours follow, taking up eighty pages. Then a week's confession, in

[*Photo, T. Mackinlay.*

A SYRIAN RURAL DEAN, CALLED A KORE-EPISCOPA, KATTANAR OF RANNI CHURCH.

preparation for the Eucharist, thirty-three pages; Eucharist, seventeen pages; the Decalogue and the Penitential Psalms, seventeen pages; and for certain special seasons, forty pages.

The Jacobites use the same devotions, but theirs are tainted with prayers to the saints and angels, and the "Hail Mary" (including, "Pray for us now and at the time of our death"), etc. In the book used by the Reformed Syrians there is, I believe, nothing remaining that an Evangelical Churchman could rightly call superstitious; at the same time it is Oriental. Thus we Missionaries have evangelised, taught in our own schools and churches the truth of the Gospel, and have left the Syrians to reform their own Rituals.

The Syrians call the Holy Supper or Holy Communion by the name of *Kurubāna*, which is equivalent to "Corban" (St. Matt. xv.), and means *The Offering*. This is a primitive word, corresponding to the Greek *προσφόρα* or *ἀναφορα*. They have the Liturgy of St. James. The Rev. G. B. Howard, quoted in Whitehouse's *Lingerings of Light in a Dark Land*,[1] gives the following preface or rubric in his translation of it:—

> "*The Anaphora of Mar James the brother of our Lord. And this is the first Corban which he said he heard and learned from the mouth of the Lord. And he did not add or omit in it a single word. And it is proper to offer this on the day of the laying on of hands, that is the giving of the degree. The new priest also should offer this Corban first. On the Lord's day moreover it is proper to offer this.*"

---

1 Brown & Co., Old Broad Street.

CHAPTER XV.

MANUSCRIPTS, SYRIAC AND MALAYALAM, AND THE PRINTED TRANSLATIONS OF THE SCRIPTURES

When Dr. Claudius Buchanan visited the Syrian churches in 1806, he was very anxious to have a translation into Malayalam made from the Syriac, which, in India, was a language known only to the clergy. There existed one Gospel in Malayalam, that of St. Matthew, and it was in manuscript, preserved at the present time in Mavelikara.

The translation, which was planned by Buchanan, in consultation with the Syrian Metropolitan, Mar Dionysius, was carried out chiefly by Philippos, a kattanar or priest, who, as deacon, wrote out with his own hand the four Gospels in Syriac some hundred and forty years ago. His name is revered amongst his people as Ramban (or monk) Philippos. When Dr. Buchanan visited Travancore a second time, in 1807, as he tells us in the *Christian Researches*, the Syrian "Bishop prosecuted the translation of the Scriptures into the Malabar language without intermission until he had completed the four Gospels." Dr. Buchanan also tells us that he himself "carried the manuscript to Bombay to be printed, an excellent fount of Malabar types having been recently cast at that place. Learned natives went from Travancore to superintend the press." Therefore just a century ago it was being laboriously set up under the eyes of the "learned natives." It is of this edition that Henry Martyn, the great missionary, in his journal,

Reads right to left.

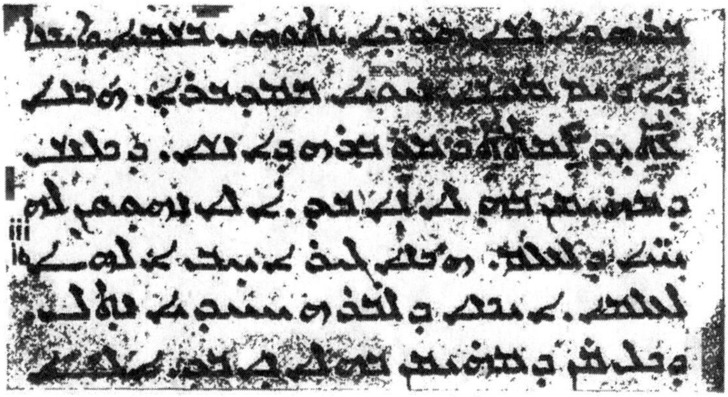

Somewhat reduced.] [*Photo, Abbott, Lindfield.*

ST. JOHN III. 16.

Syriac Manuscript of four Gospels and Acts, copied about 140 years ago by Ramban (Monk) Philippos, who afterwards, in 1806-1807, translated it into Malayalam.

under date 22nd February, 1810, writes from Bombay, saying: "At the 'Courier Press' I saw the Malayalam New Testament in print as far as the 11th of John." This, I believe, is the only version of the Scriptures ever made by Indian Christians alone, without immediate European supervision.

To quote from some words of mine written in 1892:—

"It is a very quaint translation from its close adherence to the Syriac. It never says merely Jesus, but 'Lord Jesus.' The Jewish Sabbath is always called 'Saturday.' 'Satan' is 'Akal-karusa'; Syriac, 'the slanderer'—literally, 'the devourer of flesh.' 'Leave there thy offering on the altar,' reads

Reads left to right.] [*Photo, Abbott, Lindfield.*

FIRST PRINTED MALAYALAM GOSPEL.

Specimen of type made in Bombay, 1806. The last four lines are St. John iii. 16: "God so loved the world as to give His only son." Syrian version.

Matt. v. 24. 'Give bribes' corresponds to 'show diligence,' in Luke xii. 58. 'The Father' and 'The Holy Spirit' are called by the Syriac names. 'Paraclete' or 'Comforter' reads as 'The One who refreshes or cools.' 'High Priest' is translated by the local word for 'Bishop'; the idiom of every verse is a study and a curiosity."

The following is ($\frac{1}{8}$ size) the English title-page :—

THE NEW TESTAMENT

OF

OUR LORD AND SAVIOUR

JESUS CHRIST

TRANSLATED INTO THE

MALAYALIM.

PART I.

CONTAINING THE FOUR GOSPELS.

BOMBAY:

PRINTED AT THE COURIER PRESS.

1806.[1]

The Malayalam is a curious copy of the English, and reads :—

THE NEW CONNECTION

OF

OUR LORD THE SAVING ONE

YESO MESIHA

TRANSLATED INTO THE MALAYALAM TONGUE.

THE FIRST.

CONTAINING THE FOUR EVANGELS.

---

[1] The figure is torn off my copy, but in the Malayalam the date is 1806—*i.e.*, the date of its inception. 1811 was the probable date of finishing it.

From the printed second report of the Calcutta Auxiliary Bible Society it is plain that this remarkable book was printed at the expense of the British and Foreign Bible Society.

Five years after this was published the Reverend Benjamin Bailey had arrived in Travancore, and, before long, saw the necessity of a whole Bible

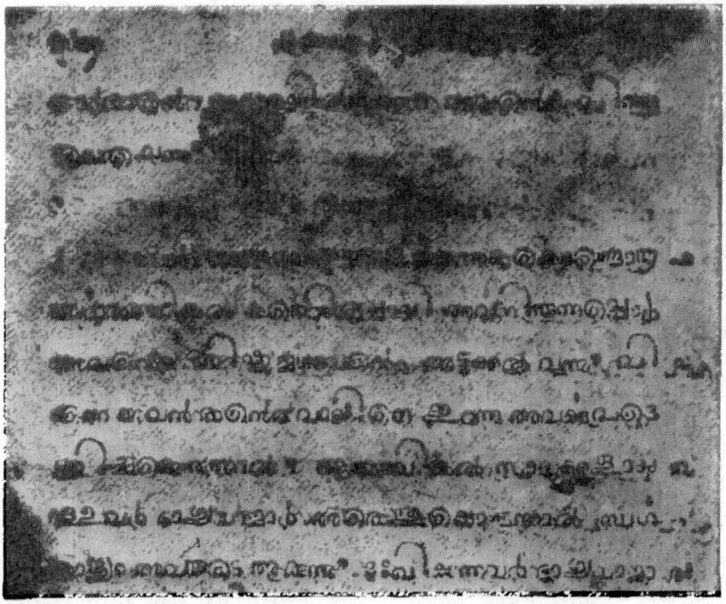

Reads left to right.] [*Photo, Abbott, Lindfield.*

SECOND PRINTED GOSPEL, ST. MATTHEW V.

(Half-size of original.)

Printed at Cottayam, with type made by Rev. Benjamin Bailey, before 1829. The press still stands, and was made by Mr. Bailey. (See page 107.)

in the vernacular, and set about the work, giving the people a new translation from the original Hebrew and Greek.

In order to secure the co-operation of the Syrian priests, he caused copies of the parts as they were translated to be made, in the native way *on palm leaves*, and these he circulated among them.

I once had one of these palm-leaf copies lent to me by Benjamin Bailey, junior.

This translation was published in 1829, but a Gospel appeared earlier, that of St. Matthew, in type cut by Mr. Bailey's native blacksmiths, and

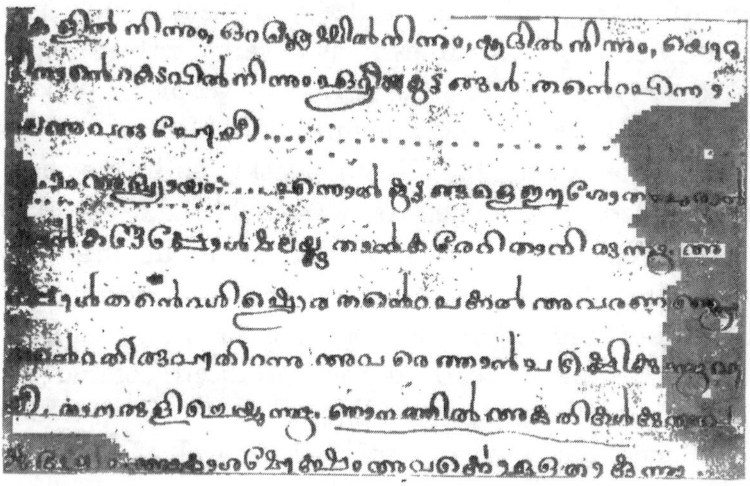

Reads left to right.] [*Photo, Abbott, Lindfield.*

COPY OF MANUSCRIPT, MALAYALAM, OF ST. MATTHEW, BEFORE 1816.

(Reduced, half-size of original.) See page 108.

printed in a press made under his directions from a description given in the *Encyclopædia Britannica*, and which is still shown in Cottayam. From our reproductions one can easily see the vast improvements made in the hundred years just past. First, there was only the Syriac, in its beautiful script, embodying the words learnt by God Incarnate when He humbled Himself to be a boy;

yet, to these natives of India, a *dead* language. Then the precious hand-written Malayalam, a living tongue, and capable under the Holy Spirit of giving life, but only a manuscript. This was followed in 1811 by the four Gospels, translated by the priests from their Syriac, and printed in the clumsy type which was thought beautiful a century ago, and had, indeed, a beauty in its wide-spreading usefulness, as every setting up of the type meant thousands of copies. Next we have Bailey's first attempt, of which my old friend, the Venerable Koshi Koshi, told me he remembered how, when it was published eighty years ago, people would crowd at night into a house and sit round a native lamp of primitive shape and dim light far into the morning, while one of the party read to the entranced company in their own language the Divine story. The Old Testament books were especially novel to them. Finally, we arrive at the Union version of the New Testament, finished in 1898. This, with the revised Old Testament, is now the valued Bible for the Malayalam people, amounting to over four millions in British and native territory, and read constantly by four hundred thousand Indian Christians. The Four Gospels in the first printed edition (1811) weighs 3 lbs. 2 oz.! and is 9½ inches by 10½ inches. The whole of the New Testament of to-day is 7½ inches long and 5 inches wide, and weighs 6 oz. Still, we are some way off from a pocket edition of the Bible. However, as the bulk of the Malayalam people have no pockets, perhaps it does not much matter.

It is but just to say that scholars, both European and Indian, representing Anglicans, Syrians, Nonconformists, and German Evangelicals,

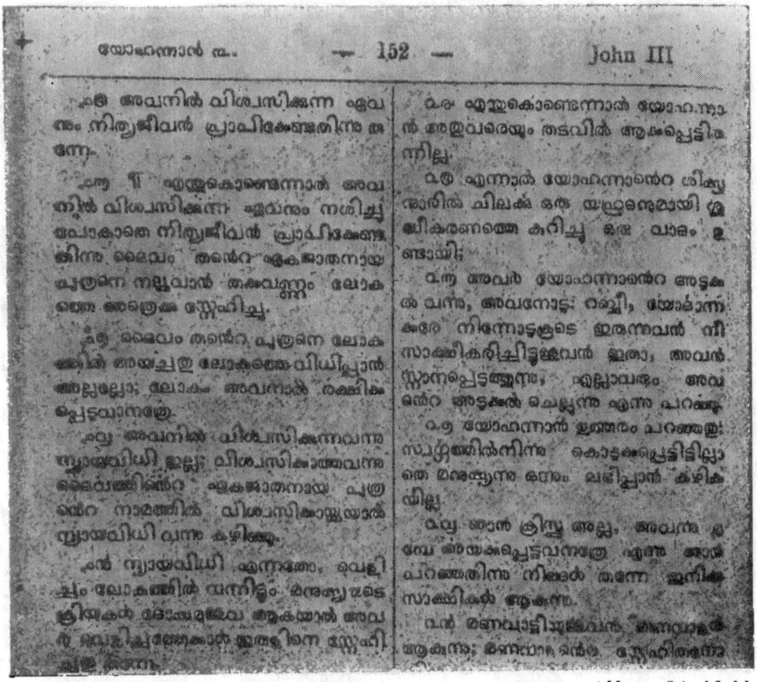
— 152 — John III

Reads left to right.] [*Photo, Abbott, Lindfield.*

REDUCED MODERN SPECIMEN OF (REVISED) NEW TESTAMENT IN MALAYALAM.

Printed at Cottayam Press.

have borne their part in giving the whole Word of God in excellent Malayalam to the people of the Malabar coast. This has been the food of revivals; one took place among the Syrians in 1874 and 1875, producing much amendment of life and much reading of the sacred Scriptures. Another revival is taking place just now, as these pages are being printed, and it seems as if the Syrians were paying back to the Church Missionary Society some of the spiritual help received by them in years gone by, for the chief agent in this revival is a Syrian layman. He goes about preaching all

[*Photo, Abbott, Lindfield.*

PHOTOGRAPHED FROM RUBBING OF A STONE MONUMENT IN THE CHINESE PROVINCE OF HSI-AN-FU.

(Containing a history in Chinese of the arrival and establishment in China under imperial protection of a Nestorian Colony, A.D. 636-781, which lasted for 145 years.) This portion contains names of Clergy in Syriac and Chinese. The Syriac in the top, reading from right to left, is *Mar Yuhannan Episkopa.* The next line is *Isaac Kashisha* (Kattanar), Priest. The fifth line is *Givargīsa* (Georgios, George), Priest. See p. 113.

over the country, and has been the means of arousing many people in the Church Missionary Society stations.

If, as we have said, the Scriptures are the food of revivals, revivals increase the demand for

Scriptures. Sometimes it has been difficult for the Mission Press to print books with sufficient speed, and while an edition of five thousand copies has been coming out, it has had to be increased to seven thousand five hundred. The British and Foreign Bible Society has thus been a true friend to the Christians of St. Thomas, and the debt is gladly acknowledged. The first reforming Metran, at his death in 1877, left Rs.50 to the Bible Society, and many of its warmest supporters are found among the Syrian priests and laymen.

CHAPTER XVI.

The Present and the Future

God's providence is very visible in the preservation of the ancient Christians of Malabar. At the very time that our King John was pulling out Jews' teeth to make them surrender their treasures, Hindu princes were protecting Jewish and Christian subjects whose ancestors had been honoured by Royal grants for hundreds of years. True, the usefulness of the immigrants would recommend their being protected, and their non-aggressiveness towards the heathen religions would ward off attack. They have resisted unto blood Roman bondage, and have been spoiled of their church endowments rather than lose the truth held by the Church of England and other reformed bodies. Can it be that Christians so preserved have no further use in God's economy? Are they saved only for themselves? Is there no purpose in their honoured position and their acclimatization in the great non-Christian land of India? Have they suffered so many things in vain? Their witness to the ancient creed of Christianity, to the Sacraments of Christ, to the form of public worship, to the identity of the Scriptures in the Churches of the

East and West, to the primitive and episcopal form of Church government, to monogamy, and to a pure family life, all combine without doubt to qualify them for great services in the future to the Church of God.

If the few hundreds who joined the rejected missionaries in 1837 have so signally helped to bring the heathen of Travancore into the flock of Christ, what may we not expect from the sixty thousand reformed members of the Church of St. Thomas under their own bishops? Their life is already telling upon the Jacobites, who, like themselves, are permitted to read the Bible in the vernacular. When the elation of the latter, winners in the long-drawn-out lawsuits for the church property, has toned down, and the depression of defeat has given place in the Reformed to the joy of freedom and the delight of progress, may we not expect union? Will not their missionary zeal, confined at present to the Malayalam States, carry them to other parts of India? The Syrians are not wealthy as English people count wealth, but if they have the means of support, Syrian evangelists will yet show that they are of the enterprising stock of which sprung Thomas the merchant and that Nestorian colony of clergy and lay-folk which braved the Indian Ocean to revive the Christianity of Malabar, and which crossed the wilds of Asia to give the Gospel to China, as recorded in Syriac and Chinese on the thousand-year old monument of Hsi-an-Fu (see page 110).

In the last century Travancore has seen the

learning of the Rev. George Matthan and of the Venerable Archdeacon Koshi, D.D., the saintliness of Archdeacon Mamen and of the Rev. K. Kuruwilla, the pastoral efficiency of the Rev. Jacob Chandy, senior, and of the Rev. Ambatta Thoma—to mention only some names of the holy dead. They were the heart of the Anglican Church in Travancore, and the stock is not exhausted; some of their sons are found already in places far distant from Malabar. Let us pray that God will still bless His Holy Word until, in the power of a risen life, the Syrians shall be to India in spiritual things what their distant cousins, the Parsees, are in things temporal. The Spirit of God can surely enable them to rise above the enervating influences of the Malabar climate.

Many can bear witness to the independence, integrity, temperance, and growing enterprise of the Syrian youth. It must prove true of them in Christian good works: "Thy people offer themselves willingly in the day of Thy power." "Thy youth are to Thee as the dew" (Ps. cx. 3., R.V., and margin). God grant it!

P.S.—After these words were written, I received unexpectedly from India two copies of *The Star of the Malankara (Malabar) Church*, the Reformers' monthly magazine, which I had not seen for two years. Among other articles, they contain a translation of "The High Priesthood," an address at the Keswick Convention by the Rev. Hubert Brook, an historical article on their Reformation by the

REV. K. M. MATTHAI, MY OLD ASSISTANT AT ALLEPPEY.

His full name is Kaipurēdatha M. Matthai. The first word is the house name or surname. " M " stands for his father's baptismal name, and " Matthai " is his own. His wife is the daughter of the late Archdeacon Oomen Mamen. The picture is given to illustrate the type of Syrian features.

Very Rev. Kattanar Aypu Thoma, Vicar-General,[1] and others on kindred subjects by Syrian graduates.

What is most interesting is the announcement of their annual convention in the usual place in the dry bed of the Ranni river. The Rev. T. Walker, of Tinnevelly, is the chief speaker, and Mrs. Nicholson and Miss McKibbin, two English ladies working among them at their own charge, have promised to address special meetings of women.

After an appeal for prayer for the Divine blessing and presence, and that they may at length rise to their duty, not only of evangelizing Malabar, but other parts of India, the Syrians who intend to be present are reminded of special collections to be made for the Bible Society, the Sunday School Society, and, last but most important of all, for the raising of Rs.1,200 to carry on for one year evangelistic work in Hyderabad, a kingdom in the northern part of South India—the Nizam's dominions.

The *Star of the Malankara Church*, March, 1908, says that the two ladies mentioned above have decided to build at once a school for Syrian girls in the town of Tiruwilla.

"It will aim at the training of girls to become good wives and mothers according to the customs of the Syrians. . . . The widow of Sub-Judge P. J. Ittyera will act as mother to the girls, and her sister, Mrs. Thomas, will help her in this excellent work. These honourable women, proficients in Western

1 Second sitting figure to the right in group of Reformers, p. 47.

education and culture, are devoting their lives, without salary, to the training of girls of their own race, through them to raise their people. . . . How thankfully we should praise our God."

✠

A PRAYER

O Almighty God, Lord of the harvest, Who didst in old days lead Thy Apostle to preach the Gospel in India, and didst enable him to set up for Thee an ensign in that land still heathen, we thank Thee for what Thou hast already wrought. Send forth labourers into Thy harvest.

Bless with Thy Holy Spirit all who seek to make known Thy Gospel everywhere, and give them good success.

Especially grant His grace more and more to the ancient Church of St. Thomas in Malabar. Bless all the bishops and clergy there, whether Syrians, Romans, or Anglicans, that they may lead Thy people into the unity of the faith and of the knowledge of the Son of God, and so bring about the conversion of those still in darkness; we ask it for the sake of Jesus Christ our Lord. Amen.

APPENDIX

SUBSTANCE OF REMARKS MADE IN A CHARGE

Delivered to the Rev. Missionaries at Cottayam on the Coast of Malabar, Monday, February 13th, 1843, *by the Right Reverend Daniel Wilson, D.D., Bishop of Calcutta, at his first Metropolitical Visitation.*

I find you, Rev. Brethren, now in 1843, in a very different position in this Mission from that which you occupied when I was here in 1835. You were then a Mission in aid of the Syrian Church on the coast of Malabar. You were acting in compliance with the wishes of the Metran and the other ecclesiastical authorities in the Syrian Diocese. You were preaching at their request in the Syrian Churches. You were translating the Scriptures, establishing schools, and assisting in the improved education of the clergy at the college founded by the exertions of Colonel Munro, the late Resident of Travancore, and in concurrence with the Metran. All these efforts had been proceeding for fifteen or twenty years most properly and justly, on the well-grounded hope that the Syrian Church, aided by your advice and example, would gradually and silently reform of itself any errors of doctrine and practice, with which lapse of time and her vicinity to the Roman Syrians had infected her.

You were perfectly right and discreet in taking this course. An independent, ancient Episcopal Church like that of the Syrian Malabaric, when discovered by the pious labours of the late Dr. Claudius Buchanan in 1806 (that is, as soon as Lord Wellesley's victories had tranquillized the south of India), was to be treated, as you have treated it, with the utmost deference, with no pretence to authority, no haste, no intermeddling, no openings given to schism, no attempts to bring it to a conformity to our own particular ecclesiastical polity; aid only was to be afforded in a spirit of love, as by one Episcopal and Scriptural Church to another, peaceably and orderly.

The somewhat sanguine view which Dr. Buchanan took of the doctrine, liturgy, and discipline of the Syrian Church has sometimes been spoken of with surprise. I venture to say that such a view was not only excusable, it was natural, it was almost necessary. The reception which that eminent person met with from the then Metran, the eagerness with which his proposal of printing the Syrian Scriptures and translating them into the vernacular tongue was welcomed, the lamentations over the declining state of the Church which were freely made, the general orthodoxy, so far as he had been informed, of their Liturgy, the episcopal polity which prevailed, and their total rejection of the pretended supremacy of the See of Rome, all led Dr. Buchanan to hope that the help and co-operation of the Episcopal Anglican Church might not only lead to the gradual improvement of the Syrian Church itself, but also make it a noble instrument for Christian Missions throughout Southern India. A union with the Church of England Dr. Buchanan, I believe, never thought of. Co-operation with it he did. He disclaimed authority, however, most distinctly in all respects, and only gave advice.

The testimony of the learned and excellent Bishop Middleton, in 1816, ten years later, is substantially the same with Dr. Buchanan's, though somewhat more reserved and cautious, as it was natural it should be, from the rank and authority of a Bishop in the Church.

The report also of La Croze, who wrote in 1724, about eighty years before Dr. Buchanan, and who drew his materials from the reluctant confessions of the Romish historians, themselves contemporary with Archbishop Menezes in 1599, is quite consistent with these more recent testimonies.

It is important, Rev. Brethren, for you to remember all this, in order that you may feel assured that the course which you took was the wise and correct one, and that you may still nourish hopes of a gradual and willing reform, at some more favourable moment than the present, when, as I shall immediately state, your connection with the Syrian Church, as a Church, has been dissevered by the act of the Metran, and you have abandoned, and necessarily abandoned, an attempt which is for a time hopeless, but which may at any moment be resumed.

Let us, then, ever bear in mind the many important points in which the Syrian Churches differed, and now differ, from the Church of Rome. I speak not of the actual opinions and practices of too many, as since discovered, but of their ecclesiastical documents, their creeds, and the faith of their more enlightened Metrans and clergy at the time of La Croze, of Dr. Buchanan and Bishop Middleton, and even now.

1.—They rejected as a Church, as they reject still, the supremacy of the Pope.

2.—They acknowledge the supreme authority of the Holy Scriptures.

3.—They hold no traditions as of co-ordinate rank with the Scriptures, and necessary to their just interpretation.

4.—They allow the Scriptures to be freely translated without comment, and read by the people.

5.—They object not to prayers in a known tongue.

6.—They do not receive the decrees of the Council of Trent.

7.—They do not hold, as a Church, transubstantiation, whatever many—too many—individuals may do.

8.—At the time of Archbishop Menezes they held only three Sacraments—Baptism, Orders, and the Supper of the Lord. When Bishop Middleton visited them, however, they admitted seven.

9.—They do not hold purgatory nor prayers for the dead, though the Metran told Bishop Middleton that the clergy, from their poverty, too much encouraged the latter of these : prayers for the dead.

10.—They do not deny the cup to the laity, though in practice they unite the elements by dipping the bread in the wine.

11.—They do not enforce celibacy on the clergy.

12.—They allow not images in churches. When that of the Virgin Mary was first exhibited in 1580 or 1590 by a Jesuit priest, the whole congregation rose up and cried out, "Away with the idol! we are Christians."[1]

13.—They allow all orthodox Churches to be branches of Christ's Holy Catholic Church.

14.—They hold, as a Church, the Canons of the First Council of Nice, A.D. 325, as well as those of Constantinople, A.D. 381, and Ephesus, A.D. 431, rejecting only those of Chalcedon, twenty years later.

15.—The numerous errors and superstitions which have crept into their Liturgies and ceremonies (which I shall immediately notice), have not been drawn out into canons and articles of faith,[2] as

---

[1] This was in their Nestorian days.—W.J.R.

[2] Probably the common people believe like Anglicans on the question of the union of the Divine and human natures of our Blessed Lord; but I have seen a very dangerous *monophysite* pamphlet which issued from the Jacobite Seminary at Cottayam.—W.J.R.

by the Church of Rome at the Council of Trent, nor bound by Anathemas on the consciences of men.

16.—They thus hold, as a Church, no sinful terms of communion, properly speaking, as the Church of Rome does, whatever their common practice may be.[1]

Keep in mind, also, my Rev. Brethren, that besides all these points, which include every question almost between the Protestant Churches of Europe and the Church of Rome, the following particulars are to be noticed:

1.—The Syrian Church presents an undeniable instance of an ancient Church, preserved for sixteen or seventeen centuries on the coast of Malabar, which has never admitted the pretended supremacy of the Roman Pontiff, nor of his peculiar dogmas; but stands a witness, like the Churches of Haute Dauphine and the Valleys of Piedmont,[2] to the comparative novelty of the usurpations and idolatry of Rome.

2.—The Church exhibits, further, an independent testimony to the apostolical polity of the Church in the threefold order of bishop, priest, and deacon, as sketched by St. Paul in his Epistles to Timothy and Titus, and deducible from St. John's Epistles to the Angels of the Seven Asiatic Churches,

[1] These sixteen points I again submitted in February, 1843, as I had in November, 1835, to the Senior Missionary, who has now been twenty-seven years on the spot, and he confirmed the accuracy of my statement.

[2] To which may be added the Syro-Chaldean Christians just reported to us in Kurdistan.

written sixty years after the promulgation of the Gospel, and uniformly acknowledged by the ecclesiastical writers of the age immediately next to that of the Apostles. No mean confirmation, this, of the Divine origin of Episcopacy, and which, surely, throws the burden of proving the contrary, if it can be proved, on our opponents.

3.—The immense value of Liturgies, Creeds, Canons and Articles of Religion, also, in securing some knowledge of the great doctrines of the Holy Trinity, of redemption by the blood of Christ, and sanctification by the Holy Spirit, through long ages of darkness, is hereby demonstrated, and, generally, the use of Liturgies from the very earliest ages is established.

4.—Again, the Syrian MSS. confirm the important fact of the integrity of our Western copies of the Scriptures.

5.—The existence of this Oriental Church, moreover, with its native bishop, priests, and deacons, its Liturgy, its Scriptures in Syriac—*i.e.*, in the then vulgar tongue (the same language as that used by our Blessed Saviour), its parochial order, its churches, with rooms for the clergy, etc., and many other of its wholesome primitive usages, proves the possibility of training a native ministry to conduct and rule ultimately the churches formed in our Missions.

6.—The Syrian Church stands a memorable proof of what Popish tyranny, intrigue, cruelty, oppression, and chicanery, with its Jesuit myrmidons, aims at when it meets with Churches not acknowledging its supremacy; the object of Rome is not to aid, to enlighten, to reform such a Church, but to dissever it from its proper bishops, to alter its Liturgy, to destroy its ancient MSS., and subdue it to the Romish yoke. The history of the proceedings of the Popish emissaries for more than one hundred and fifty years—from 1505—towards the unoffending Syrian Christians, is a specimen of the spirit which has ever animated, and animates still, that apostate body.

In what strong contrast with these machinations did the conduct of Dr. Buchanan stand out in 1806, that of Bishop Middleton in 1816, and the Church Missionaries now for nearly thirty years! These holy men, in the true spirit of Christianity, have been simply aiding with advice, and multiplying schools and copies of the Holy Scriptures, as the best means of gradually restoring the full light of the Gospel. You, my Rev. Brethren, have continued uniformly pursuing this only safe course. When I was here in 1835, the points which I found you had been aiming at, with the approbation of the Metran, for a series of years, were these five:—

(i.) The multiplying of copies of the Syrian Scriptures.

(ii.) The translation of the Scriptures into the vernacular Malayalim.

(iii.) The establishment of schools on Scripture principles.

(iv.) Improved means of education for the clergy.

(v.) The preaching and expounding of the

Gospel by sermons, in which the reverend missionaries, as they acquired the vernacular language, affectionately and cautiously aided them, at the Metran's request.

I now come to consider, as my duty compels, the causes of the unavoidable separation of our Church Mission from the Syrian Church as a body, at least, for a time. These have been the following:—

(i.) The corruptions and superstitions which you found to pervade in practice the worship and religious usages of the Syrians as they became better known to you.

(ii.) The discovery of their use of idolatrous prayers in the churches.

(iii.) The Simoniacal proceedings which were alleged against the highest ecclesiastical authorities in ordinations openly purchased and multiplied without examination of the individuals, so that eight or ten Kattanars were at places imposed on one parish, where two only were needed, and all this contrary to the agreement with Colonel Munro when he erected the Syrian College.

(iv.) These sources of uneasiness, which neutralized the missionaries' labours, were followed by the retractation by the present Metran of the approbation and permission which had been given to the reverend the Church Missionaries by his predecessors and by himself to aid the Syrian Churches in the ways which I have mentioned.

(v.) This step was accompanied with refusal by that Metran and his clergy, at a meeting held soon after I left in 1835, to adopt any one of the points of advice which I offered him at his own request, and, as I supposed, with his approbation, and on the footing of the arrangement made with the Church Missionaries under Colonel Munro's auspices.[1]

Lastly, a solemn oath imposed by the Metran on the clergy to have no intercourse whatever with the Church Missionaries, and a prohibition to the deacons to attend the college, concluded the Acts of Separation.

---

[1] The points suggested by me were simply matters of advice, as from one brother Bishop to another, and such as the best information which I could obtain from the long experience of the Rev. Missionaries led me to think were easy of accomplishment. I distinctly stated that I was a stranger, and had no authority but amongst my own people. But that as his predecessors; and he himself, had invited and welcomed the aid which Dr. Buchanan first offered to the Syrian Church, and which the Church Missionaries had for twenty years been rendering it, and as I had come as Bishop to visit the Presbyters of my own Episcopal Church, I conceived it to be my duty, as it was my pleasure, to consult him and his clergy as to the measures which might be thought most expedient for further carrying on these good designs. I added, that I came also as a friend whom he had two years before (which was the case) invited by letters to visit and help him. My suggestions were—

(1) That the College should be considered generally as the place of education for the clergy, according to the plan agreed upon by himself and his predecessors with the residents of Travancore and the Church Missionaries. A learned and pious clergy would thus be gradually formed.

(2) That the accounts of moneys, lands, funds, and property belonging to the Syrian churches should be audited by the resident, as complaints of malversation, whether true or not, were universal.

(3) That means should be devised for the support of the clergy, instead of their being maintained chiefly by fees for prayers for the dead.

(4) That schools should be spread all over the Syrian parishes, as had been long commenced, as funds allowed.

(5) That the Kattanars should expound the Gospel to the

Nothing then remained for you, my Reverend Brethren, but to act as you have done, under the direction and approbation of your beloved and respected Diocesan. You had no other course to take but to build churches for yourselves, to go on with your schools, to multiply copies of the Scriptures, to erect, as you have done, your own college, and to carry on an unfettered and open Mission for the good of the heathen[1] and Mohammedans generally, and of the individual Roman Catholics, Roman Syrians, and Syrians around you, who might voluntarily and peaceably avail themselves of your labours, avoiding all interference with the Metran and the authorities

---

people every Sunday in Malayalim, as the Church missionaries had been doing.

(6) Lastly, that the public prayers should be interpreted in Malayalim, in which language a Liturgy should be framed from their various Syriac ones for general use; the Syriac being now a learned language and not understood by the people. To these points the Metran, Malpans, and Kattanars promised their best consideration; approving them generally in the strongest terms, and thanking me again and again for my counsel. I added that my only object was to see the Syrian Church shine as a bright star in the right hand of the Son of Man—holding fast the faithful Word—the light of the Holy Spirit—the Atoning Blood of Jesus Christ—the pardon of sin through faith in Him—and the Holy Scriptures as a Divine and Inspired Word, and the foundation of all faith.

As the Metran and Kattanars rose to go, the Senior Church Missionary reminded them of the plan formed some years before under the auspices of Colonel Munro, the then Resident, for the benefit of the Syrian Church, which plan had been acted upon up to the period of the late Metran's death, and sometime after, with the full approbation of the Syrian Ecclesiastical Authorities. On this the Metran and the Kattanars, being appealed to by the Senior Missionary, confirmed it and said it was so.

[1] These far surpass in number the Syrians. At Mavelikara, the chief seat of the Syrian Church, there are 40,000 heathen and 20,000 Syrians.

of the Syrian Churches, and awaiting a more favourable time for resuming your system of co-operation and aid with them.

Since this necessary separation, I understand you have found that the corruptions of doctrine and worship in the practice of the Syrian Churches had gone so much further than had been suspected that little hope could remain of permanent good being done whilst those errors and idolatries were retained and defended, for they comprised, in fact, the very essence of Popery, except as to the supremacy of the Church of Rome. The great body believe in (i.) transubstantiation; (2) the sacrifice of the Mass for the quick and dead; (iii.) prayers for the departed; (iv.) purgatory; (v.) the worship of the Virgin Mary; (vi.) the adoration of saints; (vii.) prayers in an unknown tongue; (viii.) extreme unction; (ix.) the attributing to the clergy the power to curse and destroy men's bodies and souls; (x.) pictures in their churches representing God the Father; (xi.) prayers to the altar and the chancel, connected with which are—(xii.) the elevation of the host; (xiii.) the burning of incense; (xiv.) the ringing of bells at the time of that elevation; (xv.) the priests receiving the mass alone—which last usage, connected with auricular Confession, was represented to Bishop Middleton as held by the priests with peculiar tenacity, and as being an absolute barrier against any union with our own Protestant Church.

The Progress of your Mission, Reverend Brethren, during the seven or eight years since this renunciation of you by the Metran took place, fills my whole heart with gratitude to Almighty God. You have been licensed by the Bishop of Madras, your proper Diocesan, in consequence of the decision of his grace the Archbishop, according to your long known wishes. A large number of persons was confirmed by your Bishop at his primary visitation in 1841—at Cottayam 118, at Alleppey 125, at Mavelikara 72, at Pallam also a considerable number, as well as at Cochin and Quilon. The new college, erected with the portion of property awarded by arbitration to the Church Mission, now contains about seventy pupils, some of whom are under instruction with an ultimate view to sacred office. The schools are multiplying on all hands—four at Cottayam, five at Trichoor, eight at Pallam, others at Mavelikara, containing between five hundred and one thousand children altogether, and many of them females. The circulation of the translated Scriptures, and the avidity with which they are read on all hands, are most encouraging. The congregations assembled each Sunday in your several new churches are numerous—about six hundred, including children, were yesterday at Cottayam Church alone. The six beautiful buildings erected and being erected for Divine worship at Cottayam, Mavelikara, Pallam, Alleppey, Trichoor, and Colâtta—especially the noble Gothic church at this station of Cottayam, with its roof fifty feet in height, its area ninety feet by sixty feet, and its tower seventy-five feet from the plane of site—

ANGLICAN PRO-CATHEDRAL, COTTÀYAM, HOLY TRINITY.

Built by the Rev. Benjamin Bailey, 1840. It stands on a lovely hill. Here Bishops have held Ordinations of Deacons and Priests.

are full of promise. Lastly, the general movement in men's minds, as your peaceable and pious proceedings become better known, and the Bible and Christian schools have diffused more of the truth of the Gospel amongst the people, and the contrast between all this purity and light, and the corruptions and errors of their own worship, becoming more apparent to themselves daily, may lead us to expect great things in God's good time.

I quite concur, then, with your excellent Bishop in all which he has done. I entirely approve of the principle on which he has recommended you to carry on your Missions—viz., absolute non-interference with the Syrian Church, as a Church, at present. The ancient Christians must now seek us, not we them. We sought them for twenty years; the separation was at their instance, not ours. As to individual lay-persons, our school and church doors cannot but be open to all, and our clergy will use their discretion as to admitting such as may desire it to our communion on proper evidences. This is a question which may be properly left to the discretion of the missionary in a country where no form of Christianity is established, but where the heathen authorities of Travancore afford equal protection, under the eye of the British Resident, to Christians of every name conducting themselves peaceably, whether Portuguese Christians, Roman Syrians, or Reverend Missionaries of the Anglican Church. No question is likely to arise as to Presbyters under present circumstances. Doubtless their ordinations are valid, as are those of the Church of Rome; and if any individual Presbyter should be convinced of the superstitions, idolatries, and sinfulness of the Syrian Communion as it now is, and deliberately wish to enter our pure reformed Anglican Church, it will be for your Right Reverend Diocesan to determine what evidences of sincerity, what qualifications as to doctrine, morals, and learning, what title for maintenance, and what conditions as to his sphere of duty he will require. For the rest, no attempt of anything like proselytism must be thought of, either as to clergy or laity. We must look to the gradual influence of education, the changes which God's providence may silently effect, the new Metran and new clergy, with new dispositions, who may be raised up to solicit again our aid at any moment, and the general blessings of the grace of God on our labours.

In the meantime, let me particularly caution you, Reverend Brethren, against anything which may seem to occasion schism and division; you have fallen into nothing of this sort hitherto. But the position in which you have lately been placed by the acts of the Syrian Metran is a most delicate one, and will require all that discretion which you have ever exercised. If circumstances should alter for the better, and Metrans be appointed resembling those whom Dr. Buchanan and Bishop Middleton conferred with, it will be your pleasure and delight again to co-operate with them, and in the way in which they may desire your aid. As things now are, you have my entire approbation, in concurrence with your Diocesan's, in following the course imperatively imposed on you for a time by events over which you had no control. With God is the future. With God is all success. With God is the grace which alone can make fruitful your labours. To that grace most earnestly would I commend you.[1]

[1] Since I delivered the above remarks, I have seen the statement of proceedings relating to the establishment of the bishopric of the United Church of England and Ireland in Jerusalem, published by authority, which I cannot too earnestly commend to the particular notice of my reverend brethren at Cottayam and its circle of missions. This important and authoritative document especially charges the new bishops not to entrench upon the spiritual rights and liberties of the ancient churches in Syria, Chaldea, Egypt, and Abyssinia; but to assist them, so far as they may desire it, in the work of Christian education, presenting to their observation, but not forcing upon their acceptance, the pattern of a Church essentially scriptural in doctrine and apostolical in discipline; and taking special care to convince them that the Church of England does not wish to disturb, or divide, or interfere with them; but that she is ready, in the spirit of Christian love, to render them such offices of friendship as they may be willing to receive.

GLOSSARY

Antioch—Antaki, a seaport 400 miles north of Jerusalem, and where "the disciples were first called Christians."

Cattanar, or Kattanar—Priest (Malayalam, Lord).

Cottayam, or Kōttayam—A town of about 10,000 people in Travancore, east of Alleppey (see map). The head quarters of the Syrians and of the C.M.S. Mission. The Anglican Bishop resides here, as well as the Jacobite Metropolitan.

Jacobite—Holding the error of the monophysite bishop, Mar Jacob (sixth century).

Katholikos—The title given to certain superior bishops in the Eastern Church.

Malayalam—A South Indian language of the Dravidian family, akin to Tamil and Telugu.

Malpan (Syriac)—Teacher, professor.

Mar—Syriac for Lord, as in *Maran-atha*, "our Lord cometh," and the Eastern title of all bishops. Among the Jacobites, and elsewhere, certain sees have dynastic or official names for their bishops. The Patriarchs of Antioch are always called Mar Ignatius; the Patriarchs of Jerusalem rank next, and take the name of Mar Gregorius. The chief Jacobite Bishop of Malabar is called Mar Dionysius. Among the Reformed Syrians the present Bishop is Titus Mar Thoma, or Mar Titus Thoma. Similarly, Mar Matthew Athanasius and Mar Athanasius Matthew are the same person. In his lifetime he was known as Mar Athanasius. In the one case *Titus*, and in the other *Matthew*, are the baptismal names.

Mārāmannu (pronounced Mā-rā-man-ao)—A village on the river Ranni (Rā-nee).

Metran (Syriac)—Bishop, used interchangeably in Malabar with "Metropolitan."

Monophysite—Holding one nature, the error of those who say that there is one only composite nature in our Lord: practically only the Divine.

Nasrani—Nazarene, *i.e.*, Christian.

Nestorian—Holding the error of Nestorius that the Man Jesus became Son of God only at His baptism.

Patriarch—Bishop of one of the five great sees of Rome, Constantinople (or New Rome), Antioch, Alexandria, Jerusalem, into which Christendom was divided by the first General Council of Nicæa (A.D. 325).

Peschito, or Peshitta (Syriac)—Simple, the name given to the Syriac, the earliest version of the Greek Testament; and also the name of the whole Syriac Bible.

Rambān (Syriac)—Monk.

Syriac—A Shemitic language akin to Hebrew—almost a dialect of Hebrew, roughly speaking—spoken by our Lord. *Abba*, *epphatha*, *Eloi lama sabacthani*, etc., are Syriac words and phrases in our English Bible.

BIBLIOGRAPHY

Mostly copied from 1st Edition (1882) of Dr. Kennet's (Rev. Ch. Egbert, D.D.) Pamphlet.

Assemani Bibliotheca Orientalis. Tom. iv., pp. 391-407, 435-451.

Gouvea (F. Antonio de). *Jornada do Arcebispo de Goa Dom Frey Aleixo de Menezes Primaz da India Oriental quando foy as Serras do Malavar, y lugares em que Morão os Antigos Christaos de S. Thome —Synodo Diocesano da Igreia e Bispado de Angamale, etc.* 1 vol., small folio. Coimbra, 1606.

Geddes. *History of Church of Malabar.* 1694.

Raulin. *Historia Ecclesiæ Malabarieæ.* Romæ, 1745.

La Croze. *Histoire du Christianisme des Indes.* 2 vols., 12mo. La Haye, 1758.

Asiatic Researches. Vol. vii., pp. 364 *seq.*

S.P.C.K. Report for 1810. No. 4, pp. 187-192.

Dr. Claudius Buchanan. *Christian Researches.* 1814.

T. Yeates. *Indian Church History.* London: Maxwell.

Bishop Middleton's Life, by Le Bas-Rivingtons. 1831.

Bishop Heber's Journal. Vol. ii., with Appendix.

Archdeacon Robinson. *Last Days of Bishop Heber.* 1829.

Madras Literary Society's Journal, vol. 1834; article by Archdeacon Robinson, "Historical Account of Syrians."

"Captain Swanston's Memoir": *Journal Royal Asiatic Society.* 1834.

Professor Lee. *Brief History of Syrian Churches.* C.M.S. 17th Report.

S. Indian Christian Repository. Vol. i., 263; vol. ii., 189. Madras, 1837-1838.

Hough. *History of Christianity in India.* Vols. i., ii., and Appendix to vol. iv. (*Syrian Liturgies*).

Etheridge. *Syrian Church: Early History, Liturgies and Literature.* Pp. 538. London: Longmans.

Colonial Church Chronicle. Vol. viii. (*Christians of S. Thomas*).

C.M.S. Intelligencer. Vols. i., ii., iii., iv.

Jacob Canter-Visscher. *Letters from Malabar*. Ed. Major Heber Drury. Letter XVI. Madras, 1862.

Life of Daniel Wilson. John Murray. 1861.

Francis Day. *Land of the Perumauls*. 1863.

Howard. *Christians of S. Thomas and their Liturgies*. Oxford and London: Parker's. 1864.

Rev. Edavalikal Philippos. *Syrian Christians*. Ed. G. B. Howard (as above, 1869).

Lives of Indian Missionaries. C.K.S. 3rd series. Bishop Middleton.

The Church and the Churches in South India. 1870. Rev. J. A. Lobley. Deighton, Bell & Co.

Rev. R. Collins. *Missionary Enterprise in the East*. London: King & Co.

Lingerings of Light, &c. Whitehouse: Hamilton Adams. 1873.

Rae (Rev. G. Milne). *The Syrian Church in India*. Blackwood and Son. 1892.

Church History of Travancore, by C. M. Agur, B.A. Trevandram.

Christianity in Travancore. Mackenzie, in the Census Report of 1901. Trevandram.

Professor Legge. *Christianity in China*. "The Nestorian Monument." 1888. London: Trübner & Co.